Enriching the Young Naturalist

Enriching the Young Naturalist

The Nature of a Science Classroom

Jeff Danielian

Routledge
Taylor & Francis Group

NEW YORK AND LONDON

First published 2009 by Prufrock Press Inc.

Published 2021 by Routledge
605 Third Avenue, New York, NY 10017
2 Park Square, Milton Park, Abingdon, Oxon OX14 4RN

Routledge is an imprint of the Taylor & Francis Group, an informa business

Cover and Layout Design by Marjorie Parker

ISBN 13: 978-1-59363-377-6 (pbk)

For Samantha and Grace

Contents

Acknowledgements

I would like to thank:

- First and foremost, all of my professors at Lyndon State College, where I received my undergraduate degree in natural science. It was through the eyes of Bud Ebbett, Dave Conant, John Pellerin, Don Miller, and Michael Sherbrooke that I learned to "see" the world. Without them I would never have opened my eyes.
- The late Jim Doyle, professor of English at Lyndon State, who gave me the gift of literature.
- All of my professors at the University of Connecticut—Joe Renzulli, Sally Reis, Del Siegle, Sally Dobyns, Susan Baum, and Jann Leppien—who opened up the world of education for me and taught me to believe in myself.
- My cohorts in the Three Summers Program at the University of Connecticut, whose continued encouragement made this work possible.
- Jennifer Robins at Prufrock Press, for her insight and ideas at the beginning of this process, and careful analysis during the completion of the project.

- My editor, Rich Restaino, whose invaluable ideas, insight, and suggestions provided a level of comfort throughout the entire process of completing this book.
- Terry Neu, for my first introduction to the merging of nature and education.
- My nephew, Luke Douglas, the youngest ornithologist I know.
- My fellow educators at the PEGASUS program in Providence, RI, where I have been supported in my efforts to teach the naturalist curriculum.
- My coworkers at the National Association for Gifted Children who support all that I do.
- Elizabeth Fogarty for her expert review of the initial draft of this text.
- Loren Eiseley, for *The Immense Journey*.
- My mom and dad, who gave me the gifts of exploration, independence, and wonder.
- My sister and brother, who experienced life with me in our family.
- All of my good friends, for their unending support.
- Most importantly, my wife Samantha, my daughter Grace, and my son Cooper, the best gifts nature has ever brought to me.

Note to the Reader

If you have picked up a copy of this book, then you probably agree that science instruction needs to encompass more than mathematical formulas and memorization of terms. At its core, science implies observing, asking questions, and exploring and categorizing the natural world. To help bring this basic element of science back into the curriculum is the purpose of this book. This text presents only a small survey of the vast amount of material on teaching the naturalist disciplines. I have tried my best to clearly lead the reader through the journey of teaching students to explore, appreciate, and come to understand what it means to be a naturalist.

Because of the volume of information that exists in each of the naturalist disciplines, not much space is given to discussing the specific peculiarities of studying geology, zoology, botany, and so on. Instead, I have focused on the processes and information common to teaching students to engage in all of these studies. I have found it essential to success to allow the students to be exposed to a variety of ideas and interesting topics related to naturalistic studies; this adds an essential motivating element of choice. Information about specific naturalist disciplines can be found in many of the wonderful resources I reference throughout the book.

This book essentially is a guide to teaching your students to become naturalists. Because so many of the specifics in your lessons will be determined by the natural world in your neck of the woods, I chose not to write a unit of hard-and-fast lessons that should be followed to the letter. Besides being anathema to the spirit of naturalism, such rigidity would not accommodate variables such as time, location, and so on. In many of the chapters, I recommend a particular course of study and include handouts, assessments, and rubrics. The samples included have been successful in guiding my students; however, feel free to modify them or create your own. Other lessons are more open-ended in terms of assignments and assessments. Rather, these chapters give suggestions for activities and experiences that will support your students' journey toward becoming naturalists, leaving the specifics of instruction and assessment up to the teacher.

I am a true believer in teaching by encouragement and I often personalize all graded work with comments and suggestions for improvement, tending to stay away from strict grading methods. The naturalist discipline offers the opportunity for ascending intellectual demand. Due to the nature of the work, students who require more expertise have the occasion to attain it, and those in need of aid will receive it.

You will notice boxes titled "Teacher Talk" spread throughout the text. These present actual language that I have used with my students in order to motivate, engage, and excite them throughout the course of study. Feel free to use my words, or incorporate your own.

At the end of each chapter, I have included a list of resources and Web sites that you may find useful. Some of the references are field guides, and some are novels and collections of essays. At the end of the book I have included another list of resources, mostly books and articles that support this view of teaching and enriching the young naturalist—just in case anyone wonders what it is you're doing there in your classroom!

Remember, the young people you have in your classrooms are the future stewards of the Earth, and we need them more than ever.

Introduction

How do we as educators get students to see the beauty and wonder of what is around them in the natural world? Why must science instruction be laid out in terms of formulas, vocabulary words, and quick surveys of subject areas? Where has the exploration and discovery gone? And finally, how might we accomplish the greatest goal of all: allowing students to pursue their own interests in science in order that they might make contributions to society as a whole?

I can clearly recall the first time I taught the material presented in this book. I stood in front of the room, holding a giant sequoia pinecone I had just pulled from a box. I had asked the students to guess one object that might be hiding inside the box. A shell? A bone? A bird's nest? The look of astonishment on the faces of the students as I revealed the giant cone is etched in my mind. It presented the perfect introduction to the unit and the year. Thus began the discussion about the natural world, its hidden wonder, and how, once exposed, elements of nature take on a whole new meaning. I continue to start each and every school year with this activity. I believe it presents the essence

Having students get their hands dirty is at the heart of them becoming naturalists.

of education—wonder, nature, and mystery embedded within the curriculum.

We need a curriculum that allows children to separate math from science at an early age, one that allows them to see that science is not all facts and charts, lab reports and lab coats, data and results—a curriculum that includes every student who would like to explore, discover, and take an interest in the natural world.

The curricular guidance presented in this book is an attempt to return to the roots of science education. By allowing students to pursue an interest in the natural world, focusing on the methodologies needed to conduct fieldwork, enabling them to see and ponder the connections they perceive, and embarking upon a problem-solving approach to some naturalistic issue in their own neighborhoods, I hope that we can awaken the young naturalist, allowing him or her to understand and be aware of his or her attachment to the natural world.

Students of high ability require curriculum that not only is physically and mentally stimulating, but also enriching. This text serves as a guide to help the student "become" a naturalist in a specific field. Through in-depth study, research, and discussion, students are challenged to think creatively, solve problems, and present their work to a real audience. As a teacher of advanced-ability students, I have successfully employed the learning environment and unit presented here for the past 3 years.

In researching this text, I have sought out a multitude of guides for the naturalist, notably *The Nature Handbook: A Guide to Observing the Great Outdoors* by Ernest Herbert Williams, *Naturalist's Guide to Observing Nature* by Kurt Rinehart, and *Amateur Naturalist* by Nick Baker, all of which are wonderful guides for the discipline, but were written for an older audience. Although the tools and objectives of these books are similar to those used by the young naturalist, these texts need to be adapted for use in the classroom. I also used *Handbook of Nature Study* by Anna Botsford Comstock, which was renowned in its day as an elementary appreciation for nature, and its themes are present in this text. Two of the oldest texts that make reference to children and the study of nature are Charles B. Scott's *Nature Study and the Child*, published in 1900, and L. H. Bailey's *The Nature-Study Idea*, published in 1909.

Other texts are great for the elementary teacher and do seek to have students understand the natural world, but do not go into the depth necessary for students of high potential and ability. Examples of these include *Discovering the Naturalist Intelligence: Science in the Schoolyard* by Jenna Glock, Susan Wertz, and Maggie Meyer; *The Young Naturalist (Kid Kit)* by Usborne Books;

and *Keeping a Nature Journal: Discover a Whole New Way of Seeing the World Around You* by Clare Walker Leslie and Charles E. Roth.

In writing *Enriching the Young Naturalist*, I have been consistently aware that this text asks the reader to step back in time, walk to the outdoors, and return to the days of nature study. In its simplest form, there is not much that is required: A keen sense of observation, a place to record those observations, and an inquisitive mind are at the heart of the naturalist discipline. I wish you success as you pursue this course of instruction.

Chapter 1
What on Earth?
Getting Started

Every good unit of instruction begins with an attention-getting opening. For this unit, nothing beats a hands-on approach, much like the "show-and-tell" days of old. The more samples you can find, the better. Perhaps you have some potted plants at home, or an uncle of yours was an avid rock hound; maybe your friend happens to collect spiders. Whatever the case may be, you need to acquire a range of specimens from a variety of places. As you build this collection, keep in mind diversity and the "wow" factor, and remember that this lesson will serve as the backbone for the entire unit.

I usually bring in the giant sequoia pine cone (which I purchased at a yard sale); samples of granite, quartz, and slate collected from the woods; some spiders from the eves of the house; a giant ostrich egg; and several small plants from the local greenhouse. In the event you do not have direct access to samples, many local museums or educational collaboratives have "nature boxes" or educational kits that contain a

> "The journey is difficult, immense. We will travel as far as we can, but we cannot in one lifetime see all that we would like to see or to learn all that we hunger to know."
>
> —Loren Eiseley

multitude of specimens that you can check out for a period of time. You also can access outdoor education catalogs that have a variety of samples, mounted or preserved, for sale. When all else fails, photographs and magazine cutouts will suffice.

Once you have accumulated all that you need for this lesson, be sure to keep in mind that the goal is to stimulate thought and elicit questions. There should not be any note taking, quizzes, or the like associated with the introductory lesson. The point here is to get students involved.

When beginning a unit on natural history, ask your students if they can describe what it means to be *natural* or what it means to be part of nature. Posting student responses on the board or overhead during this short brainstorming session will help students organize their thinking about the topic. You should help guide the discussion by pointing out that the study of nature is encompassed by a number of distinct but interrelated fields. Once a sizable list has been generated, you and your students should organize that information into a knowledge tree (see Figure 1). A knowledge tree presents the structure of knowledge as it is organized into disciplines. A basic knowledge tree would list the major areas of knowledge— mathematics, logic, science, philosophy, history and humanities, and psychology—at the top. Then, branching off of these headings would be more specialized disciplines that comprise naturalism: botany, entomology, geology, ornithology, zoology, and so on. It is important for students to see how the study of nature fits into the structure of knowledge.

Once the learning tree has been fleshed out, have the class brainstorm together to identify into which discipline each of your "show-and-tell" samples falls. Depending on your own prior knowledge, you may have to research the areas listed below, as

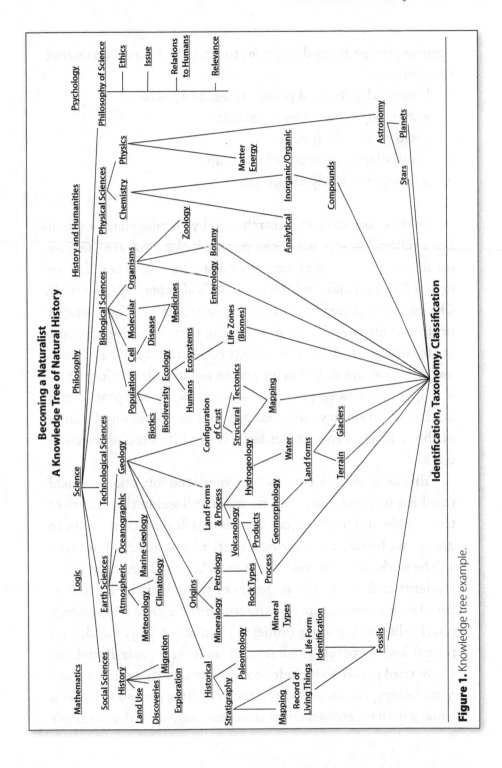

Becoming a Naturalist
A Knowledge Tree of Natural History

Figure 1. Knowledge tree example.

these are the primary disciplines that will be focused on during the unit:

- botany: the study of plants, trees, and grasses;
- entomology: the study of insects;
- geology: the study of rocks;
- ornithology: the study of birds; and
- zoology: the study of animals.

The best way to start researching is by visiting your local public or college library. The books you are looking for are the ones for science majors; two I recommend are *Procedures in Field Geology* by Tom Freeman and *Handbook of Field Botany* by Quentin D. Clarkson. Remember that we want our students to be acting as professionals would, and so accessing texts that are appropriate for college students is your best bet. Some of the best books are ones that are out of print and were published before 1950. It may sound strange, but the basic principles and practices of field observation have not changed, and the quality and beauty of the writing in these older texts is not often found in newer ones.

This unit will ask that each of your students choose a field in which to specialize. That decision will guide the nature of their study and final project. Students will sometimes work in groups with students sharing a particular specialty, but often will be working independently. It must be noted here that many students end up in subcategories of the scientific disciplines listed above. For instance, many students chose marine biology (marine life), mineralogy (minerals), geomorphology (earth landforms), and herpetology (snakes) as choices for their disciplines. I have tried before to include ecology, conservation biology, and meteorology as choices in my classroom. This proved to be problematic in the management of the classroom, difficulty of sample collection, and lack of proper instrumentation, but if you feel you can take it on, go for it!

From the moment the students select a scientific discipline in which to specialize, they begin the long journey that is presented in this book. From the outset, they will learn how to conduct themselves as professionals—learning the skills, asking the questions, and performing the duties to conduct fieldwork that will culminate in a related project. This study is naturally suited for differentiation because of the choices presented, the high-interest subject areas, and attention to individualized learning style inherent to the unit.

Teacher Talk

To get the students excited and ready to delve into the realm of the naturalist discipline, I say, "Students, you will become naturalists by the end of this unit. You will learn to think as they do, ask questions as they do, use the tools they use, and come to conclusions as they do, all while gaining an appreciation for the world outside."

I try to reiterate the point of choice here. By allowing the students to select a field, research an area of interest, and eventually develop and create a project of their choosing, they become invested in the unit.

I like to read various excerpts from the book *The Amateur Naturalist's Handbook* by Vinson Brown. The opening chapters provide great insight into the mind of a naturalist, while at the same time offering a new voice to which the students can listen. As an alternative, the students could be given a copy of the book and asked to read silently with a discussion to follow. If you are unfamiliar with the naturalist discipline, perhaps you could contact a local nature preserve, museum, or sanctuary and ask if they have any speakers who are willing to come into your classroom to give an overview of the field.

Teacher Talk

I tell students, "Naturalists do not simply collect and identify. They are observers, artists, writers, photographers, poets, curators, architects—all contributing to the field of natural history, preserving the past and opening the future."

All students then receive the form on p. 7 (see Figure 2), which may be enlarged to a size of your choosing. This form will be used throughout the unit of study and will serve as a graphic organizer for students to fill out as they move through the unit, on through the final project. Because students will be expected to keep, modify, and refer to this form throughout the unit, cardstock or heavy paper provides a great medium and students should be encouraged to write in pencil. One of the main reasons for handing this out at the onset of the unit is to get the students thinking about the many disciplines to which they have been exposed. I often have found that within a class of students, there are some who like bugs, some who like rocks, others who love plants and trees, those who enjoy fish and marine life, and still others who appreciate birds. Many, if not all of them, have never heard the correct names for these scientific disciplines. It always amazes me that a simple word like geologist, botanist, or ornithologist can stir up such emotion and excitement among my students.

Learning to Observe

Observation is a skill that is honed over time with practice. Students innately understand what it is to observe, but it always helps to delve a bit deeper into a process that most of us take for granted. I usually start with a long discussion about our senses, followed by a short 5-minute observation inside the classroom.

Naturalist Project Graphic Organizer

Name:	Naturalist Specialty:	Brief Description of What You Do:
Tools That I Use:	Questions I Ask and Things I Look for:	Interesting Ideas I Have:
Field Guide I Use:		

Project Idea:

What I Need to Complete My Project:

Student Signature:	Teacher Signature:

Figure 2. Naturalist project graphic organizer.

Naturalist Project Graphic Organizer

Please visit http://www.prufrock.com/youngnaturalist to download a full-size reproducible handout of this page.

I'll ask students to focus on their surroundings, jotting down their observations. If time permits, we travel outside for a longer observation. I have not given any formal instruction at this point and the results usually are quite interesting.

When the students have completed their observations, I ask them to share. The majority of them usually have written, "I see . . ." on their notebook pages. This provides a transition into talking about the use of all of our senses. I have them shut their eyes and focus on smelling, hearing, and touching. (I suggest that you stay away from having students explore their sense of taste, at least for now. Although it is an old wives' tale, tasting rocks is not common practice, and many a great botanist has died from tasting unknown varieties of plant life!)

The first in-class lesson usually involves me having the students sit silently, either in the classroom or, weather permitting, outside. I have them sit for 10–15 minutes, first with their eyes open, and then again with their eyes closed. Sharing of observations follows, which leads into a discussion about the use of senses.

For our first assignment, I stray as far as I can from the natural world and instead have students focus on a place at home. I tell them to find a "place" that they have never visited before within their homes, stressing the importance of safety and parental or sibling privacy. They are to conduct a 20-minute observation. Some students climb behind their TV stands while others find a corner of the dining room in which they have never sat. Other adventurers seek the top of the fridge or a darkened basement. The goal here is perspective. You could construct this lesson anyway you wish but keep in mind that when you collect the follow-up assignment, you are looking for variety in senses and also richness in descriptive words. This will help you set a baseline for all students. You will know which ones need some more assistance and which ones are ready to go off on their own.

Suggested Books

The Amateur Naturalist's Handbook by Vinson Brown

Handbook of Nature Study by Anna Botsford Comstock

Nature's Way: Observations of a Good Earthkeeper by Marion Dusoir Ennes

Thoreau's Method: A Handbook for Nature Study by David Pepi

Tom Brown's Field Guide to Nature Observation and Tracking by Tom Brown

Chapter 2

The Ultimate Tool:
Exploring a Field Guide

Perhaps the greatest tool a naturalist can possess is a field guide. Not only does it help with the identification of the sample in question, but it also serves as a reference for the entire discipline itself. In order to conduct fieldwork, a naturalist must make use of a field guide, and I constantly stress this fact in my classroom. The introduction of these types of texts is crucial at the start of a unit such as this, and so I have some individual and group assignments that follow the introduction.

When discussing fieldwork, I often joke with my students that naturalists work in the "field," and so when they go home from school and someone asks them what they have done in their day, they can answer, "We were in the field." It usually gets a laugh, but there is a point for this statement for it furthers the foundation of the student's role as naturalist.

"Even the most scientific investigator in science, the most thoroughgoing Positivist, cannot dispense with fiction; he must at least make use of categories, and they are already fictions, analogical fictions, or labels, which give us the same pleasure as children receive when they are told the 'name' of a thing."

—Henry Ellis

It is here that I stress the importance of having a field guide, a field notebook (which will be discussed later in the chapter), and something with which to write. My favorite field guides to use are the National Audubon Society field guides, although there are many others of comparable price and content, including Peterson and Simon & Schuster field guides, among a variety of others. Use your own discretion as to which field guides would work best with your students. All are available at local libraries as well as in bookstores and online. Field guides can focus on the entire United States, an individual state, or more specific regions. For example, I generally use the Eastern Region field guides. In recent times, field identification guides have sprung up online as well, and several universities offer databases of species and rock samples. The advent of technology has proven quite advantageous to naturalists and recently a brand-new worldwide database called the Encyclopedia of Life (EOL; http://www.eol.org) was launched, which not only contains a catalog of every living species on the planet, but also provides a way for new ones to be added by scientists from around the world.

Although the identification procedures and categories have not changed much over the years, the quality of field guides certainly has. It also must be noted that there are a variety of field guides geared toward a much younger audience. They provide an interesting look at the discipline, but quite often do not provide the level of detail or wealth of diversity needed for a unit such as this. If I use them at all, it is for the purpose of comparison, in order that my students may see the quality of an "advanced" field guide.

What's in a Field Guide?

There are several important features or sections of a field guide, and most, if not all, are organized in the same way. I will be using the *National Audubon Society Field Guide to North American Trees* for the following examples. It would be a good idea to acquire the guides prior to the lessons to ensure consistency and a general understanding of how they work. I have the students participate in an activity that allows them to uncover the function of each section of a field guide (see p. 15). Below you will find a quick overview of the basic contents of a field guide.

The Introduction

This provides an overview of the discipline and, quite possibly, the most important information that a student needs to become a naturalist within his or her area of specialization. Many of the answers sought throughout the unit can be found within the introduction of the field guide, which can provide key words and information for further exploration of the subject.

This tree guide shows three types of tree shapes as silhouettes, followed by the definition of a tree, a description of the various leaf types, and an accompanying silhouette key. Next is a discussion of leaf and flower parts, with a supplementary diagram illustrating the major parts of these features. Fruits are then discussed and illustrated with silhouettes. Tree habitats are briefly mentioned. The bulk of the introduction is comprised of a long discussion of the visual keys, photographs, scientific naming, and general organization of the text.

How to Use This Guide

Complete directions on the use of the guide are given in this section. The first step to using any guide is to understand how the information is organized and categorized within the text. It would help if you scan this section first, in each of the field books you are going to use in your class, before you hand these out to the students. This is to ensure that any questions that may arise will be answered quickly; the students cannot proceed unless they know how the guide is set up. All guides provide the following: a series of color plates or photographs, descriptions of species/samples, a glossary, and an index. These are discussed in detail below.

Color Plates (Photographs)

This section is extremely important and adds vibrancy to the guide. The students are always amazed by the quality and clarity of the photographs or, in some cases, colored illustrations. In our tree guide example, the plates are organized according to leaf type.

Descriptions of Species/Samples

The entire second half of the guide provides detailed descriptions of each of the species found within the book, cross-referenced with the color plates. Descriptions provide common name; scientific name; general physical description of the species, including height, diameter, leaves, bark, twigs, seeds; and silhouettes of the tree and fruit type. Next is a discussion of the habitat and range of the trees. Many field books choose to use a United States map shaded for range identification, a useful tool.

Glossary

All of the vocabulary and terms used throughout the field guide are presented here. This is of great importance because it allows the students to posses and use the language of the discipline.

Index

An index of the color plates and descriptions by common and scientific name are presented here.

Exploring a Field Guide Assignment

After acquiring a collection of field guides, you are then ready to begin a lesson about the use of the field guide. The students at this point have chosen a discipline and are ready to work with others to explore it further. Divide students into groups based on the major disciplines (e.g., a student studying snakes should meet with fellow zoologists). I use the handout on the following page, but feel free to adapt it to suit your needs.

A Professional Field Notebook

A field notebook is perhaps the second most important tool of a naturalist. Not only does it provide the user with a place to document all of his or her findings, it serves as a record of the observations made by the naturalist. There are many options for field notebooks. In past years, I have had students create their own or purchase small spiral notebooks, but I have found that the most exciting and beneficial tool is to give them a professional field notebook. It may sound odd, but the excitement exuded by students when these small, yellow, waxy-covered field notebooks are handed out is like nothing else. In bulk orders over 40, they can be purchased for as little as a few dollars a piece, a small price to pay for the excitement of your students. They are waterproof and quite compact.

Rite in the Rain field notebooks come in a variety of sizes and styles. It is up to your discretion which one to use. I choose

Exploring a Field Guide

You are to meet with your fellow -*ologists* and -*otanists* and explore the contents of your field books. You are to fill in all of the information below and answer the questions that follow.

Names of members of your group: _____

_____

_____

_____

_____

Field guide title: _____

Area of specialty: _____

1. How is the field guide organized? How do you use it?

_____

_____

_____

_____

_____

_____

2. How are the species or objects categorized in the guide?

_____

_____

_____

_____

_____

_____

Exploring a Field Guide

3. What do you think is the most helpful section in the guide? Why?

_____

_____

_____

_____

_____

4. Is there anything confusing in the guide? How so?

_____

_____

_____

_____

5. What is the coolest part of the guide? Why?

_____

_____

_____

_____

_____

6. Do you think this guide is easy or hard to use? Explain.

_____

_____

_____

_____

_____

the generic field style notebook, as it has opposing pages of lines and grids and offers a space for field notes as well as sketches. They can be purchased at http://www.riteintherain.com or at http://www.benmeadows.com.

I often stress to students that they are using actual field books naturalists in the field would use. Whether these explorers are in the jungles of the Amazon, the deserts of the southwest, or the artic tundra, Rite in the Rain field books are used. This makes for an exciting discussion.

I then show them samples of wonderfully detailed field books, both professional ones and past student work. Many of these images can be found online as well as in a variety of books related to natural history. I have provided some titles in the suggested books section of this chapter. There are several techniques to follow when completing a field entry, and I usually spend some time going over the following:

1. document name, date, location, time of day, general comment on weather;
2. heading on each new entry;
3. use of a pencil is preferred; and
4. students should fill out the table of contents when an entry is complete.

Once the students have a strong understanding of what is required for a field entry, I give them the following assignment. Again, I focus on trees for the first lessons so that I can evaluate all field notes in a similar way. Of course, if you feel that the students are ready, feel free to allow them to split into their naturalist disciplines.

The assignment is relatively simple and can be done during the school day if time permits or can be given as a homework assignment. Students are to find a tree and conduct a

20–30-minute study. They are to complete at least one sketch, write a half page of notes, and collect a sample from the tree. This might include leaves and/or fruits. The field notes they complete will be used in class as a means for identification. This will reinforce the necessity of the field guides. The amount of time you wish to spend on this is up to you, but keep in mind that, the longer students spend on basic observation, the more refined their work becomes. The rubric on page 21 applies to the lesson.

In order to ensure a careful evaluation of the authentic learning process in your classroom, carefully crafted rubrics are a must. In my years of teaching I have come to embrace rubrics, using them every chance I get. Rubrics offer students a glimpse into how they will be assessed and allow for a range of comments concerning effort, creativity, skill acquisition, and demonstration of ability. Students are able to see areas of strength while focusing on areas needing improvement.

Rubrics usually have three important areas of information: the *criteria*, or skill areas to be evaluated; *descriptors* of these criteria, which are longer statements about each criterion; and *levels of performance*, illustrating the highest and lowest levels of understanding.

I do not use the words *excellent, good, fair,* and *poor* when creating levels of performance. I prefer to relate them to the subject or discipline. For example, most of my assignments carry the following categories. *Expert in the Field* would represent the top level of naturalist work, and the lowest level, *Backyard Naturalist,* expresses that there is still work to do. with *University Naturalist* and *Student Naturalist* are tucked in between these two. Similarly, in Chapter 5, I choose to rate research on a scale of *No Stone Unturned* to *Slim.* This is simply the style I have chosen. The words *excellent* and *poor* don't pack the same authentic punch as the ones listed above. Students should never think of themselves as failures, but should look for things to improve upon. Using these types of levels lets them know it is acceptable to score in any of the categories.

Keep in mind that the goal is to allow the students to see their progress, build upon their previous work, and reflect changes asked for in the comments section. If creating a rubric is new to you, I suggest that you visit the RubiStar Web site (http://rubistar.4teachers.org/index.php) or the Authentic Assessment Toolbox (http://jonathan.mueller.faculty.noctrl.edu/toolbox/rubrics.htm). Both of these Web sites provide a wealth of novice, intermediate, and seasoned advice. RubiStar even creates rubrics for you. You can start simple, in template fashion, or work through your own ideas and criteria.

Suggested Books

National Audubon Society Field Guide to Fishes by James D. Williams and Carter Rowell Gilbert

National Audubon Society Field Guide to North American Birds by John Farrand and John L. Bull

National Audubon Society Field Guide to North American Insects and Spiders by Lorus Johnson Milne and Margery Milne

National Audubon Society Field Guide to North American Reptiles and Amphibians by John L. Behler and F. Wayne King

National Audubon Society Field Guide to North American Trees: Eastern Region by Elbert L. Little, Sonja Bullaty, and Angelo Lomeo

Tree Identification Introductory Activity Rubric

Name: _____

Sketch completed	Y	N
At least a half page of notes	Y	N
Collected sample in correct container	Y	N

Notes were written like a/an (circle one):
- ❏ Backyard Naturalist
- ❏ Student Naturalist
- ❏ University Naturalist
- ❏ Expert in the Field

Comments:

_____

_____

_____

_____

Tree Identification Introductory Activity Rubric

Chapter 3

We Can Become Naturalists!

O nce your students have been exposed to the various naturalist disciplines and have explored the field guide, it is time for them to get to work. Remember that the main goal of encouraging this type of work is to have the students "become" botanists, geologists, ornithologists, and so on. In this way, the student not only will be thinking and acting like the naturalist, but he or she also will be using the tools that one would use in the field.

Any good naturalist will tell you that authentic fieldwork is where the learning takes place, and so it is highly recommended that you plan some time for actual fieldwork. Students will use field guides as the main tool for identification purposes. They also will be introduced to a variety of tools. Nature journaling and photography will serve as a way to document their findings.

My two favorite books, *The Amateur Naturalist* by Nick Baker and *The Nature Handbook* by Ernest H. Williams, are great resources for teachers seeking to enrich the students in their classes. Even

"The way to do fieldwork is never to come up for air until it is all over."
—Margaret Mead

though these texts are written for a more mature audience, the themes and information can easily be transferred into the classroom. Each book is quite extensive in explaining what to look for when conducting naturalist excursions.

I usually start off by having students do some basic research about the common species, plants, or rock types that they may encounter when they venture out into the field, either on their own or during class time. This serves as a way to increase their vocabulary as well as their comfort level with the material. After this research, they should feel comfortable with what they will encounter. The research conducted and notes completed will then be used in creating a "fact sheet poster" that displays what they have found.

Teacher Talk

After the students finish their preliminary research, I share this information: "You are now going to have the opportunity to go into the field as a naturalist would. Equipped with the tools you need and the questions you have, you are on your way to becoming an expert in your field. Keep in mind all that we have talked about during the past few weeks, the comments I made on your preliminary field notes, and the suggestions I had for improvement. Remember that all of you excel in different areas and that this is not a competition. Simply try to do your individual best. Some of us are better writers, while others are better artists. All of us possess the ability to observe in some way, though, and that is the point of entering the field. Remember to date your entry and make note of your location. I look forward to looking over your notes. Have fun."

The assignment and rubric are shown on pages 25–26.

Common Species/Plants/Rock Types

During the week ahead, you will do a little bit of research, a little bit of documentation, and a little bit of exploring. I will be available for consultation if you need assistance.

For this assignment, you will use your field book to document five common species, plants, or rock types. You can use a variety of sources for this work—field guides, Web sites, or the numerous resource books found in the library. Remember, the reference librarian is there to help you. The goal of this exercise is for you to familiarize yourself with some common natural wonders of our state. All of your work should be done in your field notes. For each of the five "samples" you choose, you are to provide the following:

1. Three to four sentences describing the physical features of the chosen species, plant, or rock.
2. One detailed sketch that may or may not be colored. Labeling helps with size and color identification.
3. The common name as well as the scientific name.
4. Common places someone may find it.
5. Documentation of where you found this information.
6. One or more questions you may have about it.

Common Species/Plant/Rock Types Rubric

Name: _____

At least 3–4 sentences for each	Y	N
A detailed sketch for each	Y	N
Common name and/or scientific name provided	Y	N
Documentation provided	Y	N

Notes were written like a/an (circle one):
- ❏ Backyard Naturalist
- ❏ Student Naturalist
- ❏ University Naturalist
- ❏ Expert in the Field

Sketches were completed like a/an (circle one):
- ❏ Backyard Naturalist
- ❏ Student Naturalist
- ❏ University Naturalist
- ❏ Expert in the Field

Comments:

_____

_____

_____

Fact Sheet Product

It's always a good idea to vary the ways in which your students demonstrate what they have learned. Once your students have gathered information on common species, plants, or rock types in their state, it's a good opportunity for them to learn ways in which professional naturalists present their knowledge and research to others. When you go to a museum, you don't see pages of torn-out field notes behind glass cases! The next assignment asks students to turn the information in their notes into a fact sheet poster that will be attractive as well as informative.

For this assignment, I usually have students use Microsoft Word, simply because it is readily available on our school computers and most students already have a familiarity with it. However, it is not best suited as a desktop publishing program and your school may have access to better design software. You may decide to have your students create their posters by hand, using tried-and-true materials like construction paper, glue, and markers instead. However, having students complete the work on the computer will make it easier for them to find and insert images, and it also will give their fact sheets a more professional look. I have included a sample of one of my students' fact sheet poster (see Figure 3).

Regardless of the format, some basic instructions would apply. Fact sheet products should contain:

- a title,
- the student's name,
- at least three text boxes with borders—one for each sample, and
- at least two images.

Students should think of their fact sheet as a way to present the information gathered from both their observations in the

Marine Species of Rhode Island
Created by Monica Prudencio

The American lobster lives in the cold water of the Atlantic coast. Adults are approximately 9 inches long and weigh about 2 pounds. The majority of the body is encased in a mottled greenish-brown shell, called a carapace. The head contains sensory organs, such as the eyes and the two long antennae. This lobster has five pairs of legs: four for walking, and two in front which are actually large claws. Here's a weird fact about these claws: Like humans, an American lobster has a dominant claw. This claw grows larger than the other and is the crushing claw. The other, smaller claw is the pinching claw, used primarily to catch food. This is the claw a lobster will attempt to pinch you with. The lobster "swims" backward using it's tail when threatened.

Cutest seal

HARBOR SEAL

AMERICAN LOBSTER

ENORMOUS!

QUAHOG

Pretty Shell!

The harbor seal is recognized by it's short snout and round head. It has a grey to black coat with dark spots or whit rings around the back. The male and female are similar in size. They are typically between 4 and 5 ft. long and weigh 220-250 lbs. on average. The harbor seal eats over 15 lbs of food per day, but it can go for long periods without eating, surviving off it's blubber layer. They move out of water by flopping along on their bellies. They are found all along the New England coast.

The quahog is a bivalve mollusk. This means that it has a hinged shell mad up of two halves, or *valves*. The name comes from the Narragansett Indian tribe, who used the shells as *wampum*, or money. The inside of the shell is purple and white. More purple meant a higher value. If you open a quahog, you can see the adductor muscle scars on the inside of the thick shell. Quahogs were originally native to Rhode Island, but they are now found all over the East coast. They are particularly abundant from Cape Cod to New Jersey. Quahogs are often found in estuaries, such as the Narragansett Bay, because the mixing of fresh and salt water provides ideal salinity conditions.

Figure 3. Sample student fact sheet for marine species.

field and extended research. Style and attractiveness, as well as content, are essential to communicating what they have learned to others. Encourage your students to be creative!

Tools of the Trade

As with any discipline, certain tools—both hardware and the more intangible variety—are essential. The next series of lessons involves a variety of activities that seek to have the students understand the tools of naturalists. I focus on the physical tools first.

Listed below are what I have found to be the best and least expensive tools for you to use in the classroom. While talking about each of the following, it would be a good idea to have each tool on hand for a demonstration.

Binoculars and Hand Lenses

A naturalist's skill is grounded in observation. Whether it is viewing a bird or animal at a distance, or viewing a rock sample, insect, leaf, or feather up close, a trusty pair of binoculars or hand lens is crucial. These are relatively inexpensive but highly necessary.

Camera

A camera is not essential, but does serve as a great instrument for keeping a record of something you wish to view later. In this age of digital cameras, the use of one in the field is highly recommended due to the quick viewing times of images.

Collecting Tools and Containers

Every field study is unique, but every good naturalist needs tools for acquiring, and some type of container in which to store, samples. These tools include a rock hammer, a net, and a jar or a sample bag. Once you know what you will be observing, you and your students will be able to brainstorm ideas for exactly what will be needed.

Field Guides

A field guide is the naturalist's bible. It not only helps in the identification process, but a good guide also provides keys, facts, and other interesting bits of information necessary to understanding what it is you and your students are observing (Chapter 2 presented a detailed look at field guides).

Field Book or Journal

This is the naturalist's diary, where he or she records notes, documents findings, and writes personal reflections about what has been observed. The naturalist must not leave home without it.

Writing Utensil

Pencils are my favorite, and having some colored ones on hand is great, too. A permanent marker is also a good choice, especially if you are labeling a container.

Backpacks and Side Packs

It is always good to have something in which to store all of your materials.

Preparing for Field Study

After students have been given the basics on what is needed to observe and collect samples, it is time to prepare them for their first real foray into the field. Before cutting your students loose in the field, they need to learn a bit more about the kinds of things naturalists look for and the questions they ask. Going into detail about every subgroup of the naturalist discipline during class time would be both time-consuming and unnecessary for all of the students to hear. It is important to give general background information, but students will benefit more from gaining a greater depth of understanding of the big questions and concerns of their own chosen subgroup (zoologists, botanists, geologists, and so on). The sooner students can begin to specialize, the sooner they can capitalize on enthusiasm for a particular discipline. Therefore, I suggest dividing students into their chosen fields for the following assignment, "Thinking Like a Naturalist."

The assignment revolves around two specific questions: "What do naturalists do?" and "What questions do they ask?" Examining the concerns and curiosities of the specific subgroups of professionals gives students great insight into the mental tools needed when an individual practices in his or her chosen field. This assignment lends itself to varying degrees of complexity. Students with a high degree of intellect often come up with very detailed and inquisitive responses and questions. Students who require some help come up with the basic responses and questions, which are fine for them. Keep in mind that the main focus of this assignment is to get the students to start thinking in terms of their discipline areas. The worksheet I use is on page 32, but of course feel free to modify it or make your own.

As a result of the work completed, a discussion during class should yield a list similar to the one below, which outlines what the various naturalist specialists look for in the field.

- *Zoologist (Animals):* behavior, habitat, tracks, appearance, sounds, correct naming procedures.
- *Etymologist (Insects):* body types, coloring, behavior, habitat, nests or other homes, evidence of where they have been.

Thinking Like a Naturalist

Name: _____

Naturalist Specialization: _____
(biologist, zoologist, botanist, etc.)

Search the Web and/or books at the library to find the answers to the following questions. These will help guide you in understanding the roles of the naturalist field you have chosen.

1. What does a/an _____**do?** *Please write these as statements, as in, "A biologist examines life." To find more specific examples, you can simply type into a Web search, "What does a/an* _____ *do?" Try to vary your answers from different perspectives. Provide at least five statements.*

_____

_____

_____

_____

_____

2. Questions _____ **ask.** *Please write these as questions using "what," "where," "who," "why," etc. Again, you simply can type in, "Questions* _____ *ask," and you will find many ideas. Provide at least five questions.*

_____

_____

_____

_____

_____

3. List skills your naturalist would use. *For example, a geologist would use his or her research skills; a botanist needs to be patient. Provide at least five skills.*

_____

_____

_____

_____

_____

- *Ornithologist (Birds):* wing types, coloring, body and beak types, song, nesting, feeding, habitat.
- *Arborist (Trees):* leaf type, seed type, type of tree, where they grow, coloring, shapes of branches, patterns.
- *Botanist (Plants):* stalk, leafs, flowers, fruits, seeds, root types, poisonous or not.
- *Geologist (Rocks):* types of rock, types of minerals, hardness, color, commonalities, where to find, effects on ground type.

Once the students have come up with their lists of questions, they must be checked over for detail. Only then can students begin their observations in the field.

You will have to decide how long you and your students are able to spend in the field. I recommend that at least two class periods of preliminary fieldwork be completed early on, so that the students can get a feel for nature, what they are observing, and how to conduct themselves. After these initial field studies, I try to get outside with the students whenever I can. The daily schedule dictates when and how often I am able to do this. Students also are expected to conduct studies in their neighborhoods for homework.

The school where I teach has a few acres of woodland, providing a place to conduct these studies, but in speaking with many educators, I know that this is not the case for all. A small park or playground can provide a "place of retreat" for students wishing to conduct fieldwork. I know of one teacher who uses a small grassy area in the front of the school. There are a few trees, a stone wall, and bugs and birds galore. It is amazing what can be found, even in the city. Keep in mind that these are only preliminary filed studies. I suggest taking at least one daylong field trip to a nature preserve, forest, park, or other natural environment.

At the end of this chapter is a generic handout and assignment to give to your students before their first field study. It can be used for this preliminary excursion and modified for any longer trips to the field you take later on in the unit. The handout and assignment reiterates the importance of the required tools they need to bring, as well as the concerns and questions of each naturalist field. The questions on the handout will help focus students' attention ahead of time toward what they expect to find, the specimens they will be looking for, as well as the best places to find them.

Before the preliminary field excursion, you will want to make sure you and your students have acquired the necessary tools for observation and collecting discussed earlier in this chapter. Also helpful would be to provide your students with a map of the area in which they will be observing (whether it be a map provided by the local park or wildlife preserve, or a more rudimentary map you create yourself). Having a map will help students identify ahead of time the areas—tide pools, brush, woods, etc.—where they will be more likely to find the specimens they wish to observe. Of course, you will want to make some introductory remarks before heading into the field, both to clarify expectations and to motivate students. You will want to modify your remarks to suit the location of your field study, but be as specific as possible in your directions.

A Note on Evaluating Field Notebooks

You will want to evaluate your students' field books after this preliminary excursion. I grade my students' field notebooks using a rubric similar to the one used with the Common Species/ Plants/Rock Types assignment on page 26. This basic rubric can be

Teacher Talk

Before entering the field, I share the following with students: "Now that we have learned about the tools and concerns of the naturalist, it is time to go out into the field and see first hand the wonders that surround us. In order for us to get the most out of our time, it would greatly help to be as prepared as possible, meaning that you should have a good idea of what you are looking for, looking at, and collecting. Keep in mind the tools that you wish to bring. Some of you may have to modify your species or sample list depending on what we encounter out in the field. There most likely will be a lack of large mammals present, due to our presence, so zoologists should plan on studying with one of the other groups, focusing on insects, marine life, or birds.

"You will be traveling as a group of naturalists—birders with birders, geologists with geologists, and so on. It helps to be quiet and still when observing wildlife, so keep that in mind. On your assignment sheet are some points and questions to guide your observations. I want you to enjoy your time out in the field and I respect your judgment. Remember to be safe and be observant and respectful of others."

modified for any field assignment, and the consistency of using the same rubric throughout the unit will help your students gain a growing understanding of how to improve their work. To get an idea of what a thorough field entry looks like, I have included a couple of examples of my students' field book entries in Figures 4 and 5.

Suggested Books

The Amateur Naturalist by Nick Baker

Ecology and Field Biology by R. L Smith

Field Geology Illustrated by Terry S. Maley

The Nature Handbook by E. H. Williams

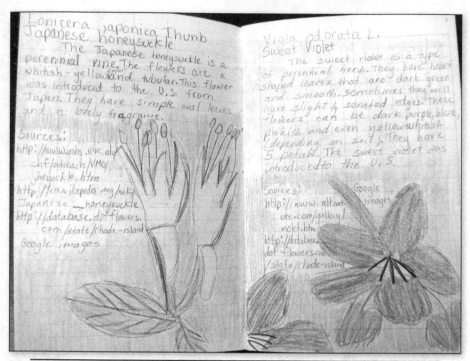

Figure 4. Sample student field notes on Japanese honeysuckle and sweet violet.

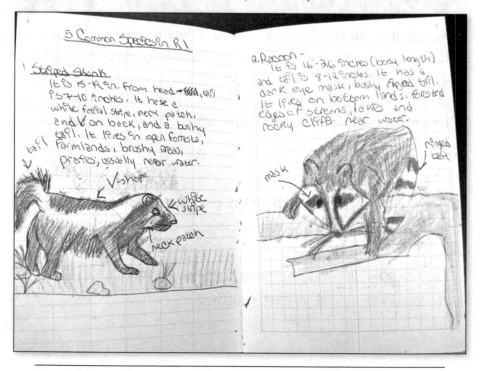

Figure 5. Sample student field notes on striped skunk and raccoon.

Field Study

Directions: Keep the following in mind when preparing to go into the field. Each group of naturalists will have different concerns and interests, but all will require the same attention to detail.

Basic Characteristics to Look for:

- **Animals:** behavior, habitat, tracks, appearance, sounds, correct naming procedures
- **Insects:** body types, coloring, behavior, habitat, nests or other homes, evidence of where they have been
- **Birds:** wing types, coloring, body and beak types, song, nesting, feeding, habitat
- **Trees:** leaf type, seed type, type of tree, where they grow, coloring, shapes of branches, patterns
- **Plants:** stalk, leaves, flowers, fruits, seeds, root types, poisonous or not
- **Rocks:** types of rock, types of minerals, hardness, color, commonalities, where to find, effects on ground type

Tools of the Trade:

- Binoculars and/or hand lens
- Camera
- Collecting tools and containers
- Field guide
- Field book or journal
- Writing utensil
- Backpack
- Map

Field Study

Places to Get Materials and Tools

Acorn Naturalists (http://www.acornnaturalists.com) caters to educators who seek prepackaged lessons and activities. They also have a wide variety of preserved and artificial samples.

The Ben Meadows Company (http://www.benmedows.com) has a large collection of tools and resources for the naturalist classroom.

Chapter 4

Museums, Zoos, and Societies of Natural History

Museums are perhaps the most common site visited on school field trips. Quite often, the students gaze around as they are rushed through the galleries and exhibits, carrying a worksheet in order to "keep them busy." The same can be said of zoos. All too often, docents (volunteers), likeable and friendly as they may, offer only a glimpse of information relating to a particular discipline. I recently watched one of these volunteers walk an entire group of seventh graders past a plaster casting of Mary Leakey's "walking floor," on which were found some of the earliest hominid footprints in volcanic ash. I stood, jaw agape, at the missed opportunity for education that was presented. I pondered how often this occurred. How many students also had walked by, never seeing firsthand the history and wonder before them?

The best way to visit such places is to accept the unguided tour. This allows you, the educator, to construct the trip in any way you wish. It also helps to reassure the museum that your students

> "Museums and scientists who inhabit them will play a key role, perhaps the key role, in the full exploration of life on earth."
> —E. O. Wilson

Museums offer students access to specimens often difficult to study up close in the field.

will be busy the entire time. It is quite fun to walk into a museum or zoo with a group of students equipped with field books, ready to work. I have found it quite rewarding to observe my students hard at work, oblivious to outside interruption. Although the text that follows relates to actual visits to a museum or a zoo, there are many alternatives, namely online content and virtual field trips. Most, if not all, major museums offer fantastic and rich Web sites, full of photographs, species identification keys, and a wealth of educational support materials. A simple search and exploration on many of these sites will uncover useful guidance and instruction. Another great alternative is to visit a local natural history museum or small nature collection. You would be surprised at how many universities, colleges, and even local libraries have natural history collections on hand, just waiting to be viewed.

Visiting the museum or zoo on your own, prior to a class visit, is quite helpful. School vacations and days off provide a relaxing and unrushed time in which to view all that the institution has to offer. Firsthand knowledge is best when conveying the overall excitement of the place to the class. The students get a sense of what to expect, and you will find it easier to spread yourself out over the course of the trip. Again, many Web sites offer maps of the premises and great supporting materials, allowing you to feel as if you are actually at the museum or zoo.

Natural history museums perhaps are the finest places to visit, given that they have such a variety of naturalist disciplines represented. There are rocks and mineral specimens for the geologists, plant and tree samples for the botanists, taxidermist specimens of animals and birds for the zoologists and ornithologists, as well as mounted insects for the entomologists. In many cases, they are organized by discipline and set aside in different rooms. This type of museum differs from a traditional science museum in that the focus is strictly on the natural world. Physical and chemical demonstrations will not be found in these halls of history. There are no tornado tubes, echo chambers, lightning bolts, or water turbines. It is exactly the type of museum that needs to be visited when teaching a unit such as this. Following the lesson and handout, you will find a list of my favorite museums and their Web sites. Have fun in your exploration!

Zoos provide another type of trip altogether. In recent years, I have strayed from the zoo for several reasons. First, there is a limited scope of disciplines present, and the geologists often feel left out. Secondly, the atmosphere at the zoo often is one of "playtime." Third, the zoo often requires chaperones to stay with all students at all times, which makes it hard to accommodate the variety of student choices. I would suggest that you plan ahead for this aspect, assuring the zoo that the students are responsible enough to work on their own. Fourth, although the zoo provides an exciting variety of species, it is more suited for a "field" trip when the students are ready to observe past the physical and move into the realm of behavior, habitat, diet, and the like. I am not saying to avoid the zoo; just be prepared when you do go there.

What follows is a sample lesson designed to expose the students to a natural history museum. Feel free to tailor it to the specific museum your classes will visit. However, many of the remarks and the assignment itself should suit any natural history museum. The goal is for the students not only to be conducting observations at the museum, but also looking at the design of a museum exhibit.

I rate the students using the same field book guidelines as I have for past fieldwork. If it is not possible for you to visit a museum, I urge you to explore some of my favorite natural history museums online. You will find the Web sites quite helpful. The University of California Museum of Paleontology on the

Teacher Talk

Before taking my students to a museum, I share my expectations for the trip: "We will be visiting the _____ Museum of Natural History. I am going to allow you to go off and explore, but be aware that your assignment is lengthy and will require time and dedication. I hope that you do take the time to visit each and every gallery. Your assignment is the same no matter what and where you choose to explore. In reality, we could spend days here, and it is my hope that you find something exciting and wish to return. This place is truly astonishing, and serves not only as a museum, but also as a working research center.

"Please note that this is not the zoo. While I know that I don't need to remind you to be on your best behavior, I am anyway. You should be absolutely silent throughout your visit unless you are speaking quietly with one of your peers, and, of course, no running, shouting, or fooling around. I also ask that you do not travel in groups of more than three people. I hope you take this visit seriously."

Berkeley Campus has a compendium of sources on its Web site (http://www.ucmp.berkeley.edu/collections/other.html). It contains links to a wealth of online collection catalogs in all of the related disciplines. Many of these lists also include identification keys, images, bibliographies, and more. I visit the site quite often and urge my students to as well. The University of Washington Libraries' Web site (http://www.lib.washington.edu/sla/natmus.html) contains hundreds of links to natural history museums all over the world. It is worth a look as well.

A visit to a museum or zoo can prove to be quite beneficial in terms of letting the students experience the "real-world" applications of their field of study. I also have included a list of virtual field trips in Chapter 10. These, supplemented with online visits to the suggested museum sites found in this chapter, would be an excellent alternative to an onsite visit.

Natural History Museum Assignment

At the Museum

Using your field books, you are to study five specimens and/or samples within your discipline area. These can be found in one gallery or from several collections. Don't forget pencils, your field book, this sheet, and colored pencils if you choose.

Each study must contain:

1. A title on the top of the page (including the gallery, specimen, etc.).
2. Information given at the exhibit, such as where it was discovered, who discovered it, and any other interesting facts about it.
3. A labeled sketch.
4. Your written observations.
5. Your interpretation and ideas (e.g., why you chose it, patterns that emerge, relationships you see).

When We Return From the Museum

Using your five completed studies, you are to write up a two-page summary of your visit that explains your overall attitude toward the field trip, what you liked best, why, and any relationships you noticed, patterns that emerged, or connections with previous work you have observed. I would also like you to comment on a particular exhibit you observed. You will hand in your field book for review along with your two-page summary.

Some more of my favorite natural history museum Web sites include:

- American Museum of Natural History (New York, NY; http://www.amnh.org)
- Carnegie Museum of Natural History (Pittsburgh, PA; http://www.carnegiemnh.org)
- Cleveland Museum of Natural History (Cleveland, OH; http://www.cmnh.org/site)
- The Field Museum (Chicago, IL; http://www.fieldmuseum.org)
- Harvard Museum of Natural History (Boston, MA; http://www.hmnh.harvard.edu)
- National Museum of Natural History, Smithsonian Institution (Washington, DC; http://www.mnh.si.edu)
- Natural History Museum of Los Angeles County (Los Angeles, CA; http://www.nhm.org)
- Natural History Museum (London, England; http://www.nhm.ac.uk)
- Peabody Museum of Natural History, Yale University (New Haven, CT; http://www.peabody.yale.edu)

Societies

One of the most exciting opportunities that I present to my students is the possibility of becoming a member of a society, association, or organization. For a small fee, students can receive journals, newsletters, online content, and even a membership card. Just by joining one of these, students receive the confidence that sometimes is needed. They feel part of a group. They feel like the *-ologist* or *-otanist*. They also learn about advocacy. Many of these societies offer student or junior memberships for less than $30, and some of them are free. If the organization or society does not have a specific K–12 student membership, many students still can become "student" members at a reduced rate (a category often specified for college students). Oftentimes a simple e-mail inquiry describing the situation will allow for K–12 students to become members of many organizations.

I usually have my students research the different societies that exist and I have them fill out a note card with:

1. the name of the society,
2. the web site url,
3. the cost of a student or junior membership, and
4. the benefits of that membership.

It often makes for a great discussion afterward, and it is good to keep these note cards on file for future use. Many of my students, I am proud to say, are members of these societies. What follows is a short list of their favorites. They are organized by discipline and include membership information.

Botany

Botanical Society of America (http://www.botany.org) charges a nominal fee for membership; benefits include a 7-year membership, calls for nominations, special newsletters, reproducible science articles, and special Web site access, a student botany newsletter, and featured educational resources.

Conservation and Environmental Issues

The Nature Conservancy (http://www.nature.org) uses a strategic, science-based planning process, called Conservation by Design, which helps us identify the highest-priority places—landscapes and seascapes—that, if conserved, promise to ensure biodiversity over the long term. Benefits include four issues of the award-winning *Nature Conservancy* magazine, invitations to field trips and special events at Nature Conservancy preserves, as well as opportunities to create a personalized nature page and receive the monthly *Great Places* e-newsletter.

Sierra Club (http://www.sierraclub.org) seeks to educate and enlist humanity to protect and restore the quality of the natural and human environment. Benefits include a one-year subscription to *Sierra* magazine; discounts on Sierra Club calendars, books, and other merchandise; and often a free gift such as binoculars or a rucksack.

Entomology

Entomological Society of America (http://www.entsoc.org) charges a nominal fee for membership; youth members receive a subscription to *American Entomologist*.

Geology

Geological Society of America (http://www.geosociety.org) charges a nominal fee for membership; benefits include science journal, online access and archives, news and items of interest, and science and news magazines.

General Science and Natural History

Society for Amateur Scientists (http://www.sas.org) is a nonprofit research and education organization dedicated to helping enrich people's lives by taking part in scientific adventures of all kinds. Benefits include the biweekly electronic magazine, *The Citizen Scientist*, and access to an online community of scientists.

The Society for the Preservation of Natural History Collections (http://www.spnhc.org) is an international society dedicated to preserving, conservation, and management of natural history collections. Benefits include the *Collection Forum*, a biannual journal, and two issues of the *SPNHC Newsletter* each year.

Herpetology and Ichthyology

American Society of Ichthyologists and Herpetologists (http://www.asih.org) charges a nominal fee for membership; benefits include a subscription to the society's journal, *Copeia*.

Mammalogy

International Primate Protection League (http://www.ippl.org) charges a nominal fee for membership; benefits include a subscription to its publication.

The Mammal Society (http://www.abdn.ac.uk/mammal) charges a nominal fee for membership; benefits include taking part in the Mammal Action Summer Expedition, where students can discover how to watch, record, and conserve mammals.

Ornithology

The American Ornithologists' Union (http://www.aou.org) charges a nominal fee for membership; benefits include participation in the leading scientific ornithological association of the Western Hemisphere, subscriptions to *The Auk* and *Ornithological Monographs*, both available online and/or in print, as well as The Birds of North America Online.

National Audubon Society (http://www.audubon.org) charges a nominal fee for membership; benefits include a subscription for one year to *Audubon* magazine and a pair of free zoom binoculars.

Zoology

American Society of Animal Science (http://www.asas.org) charges a membership fee; benefits include access to the online version of the *Journal of Animal Science*.

Chapter 5

Holding a Seminar

During my undergraduate studies in natural science, I was exposed to a class called Seminar. It was perhaps the most rewarding educational experience of my time spent studying the natural sciences. Not only did it allow for the expression of ideas by all members of the class, but it also helped to secure and strengthen my self-confidence. The solidification of skills learned throughout that period of study has stood the test of time, and I often find myself at times referring back to the organization, documentation, and presentation skills used.

When the time is right, and this will differ in each of your educational settings, the introduction of a seminar component is strongly encouraged. We shall discuss the logistics of organization and presentation later, but for now, let us look at the structure of a seminar environment.

In the most basic of terms, a seminar is defined as a group of people who come together to present, discuss, and ponder topics of interest related to the discipline. In some cases, the topics may be

> "Our observation of nature must be diligent, our reflection profound, and our experiments exact."
> —Denis Diderot

posted on a Web site or bulletin board beforehand, and each member comes with information to add to a discussion; in other cases, participants research a predetermined or preselected topic.

In the case of my own experience and classroom assignments, I have chosen the latter when using a seminar environment. Students submit ideas from their discipline areas and go off to research the topic. A trip to the library or a visit online can provide a wealth of research options for students.

Remember that your goal is not only to allow the students to participate in a discussion, but to actually research a given topic in a specific area of interest and present to the group at large. To this extent, the students will sort information, summarize and outline their findings, and plan a seminar discussion to be held at a later time and date.

The primary goal of this lesson is to provide the students with an avenue for research relating to their field. A seminar atmosphere can help them refine a topic and present it to the class. It also may serve as a means for them to generate new ideas and research questions.

Teacher Talk

To prepare students for the seminar, I share the following: "Class, today we are going to discuss our next assignment, the preparation of a seminar. A seminar, especially in science, is constructed so that a small group or individual is responsible for preparing a small discussion on a fine-tuned topic. The more refined and detailed the topic, the better the discussion. I will be asking you to choose a seminar topic within your chosen naturalist area."

The following step-by-step instructions should provide a guide for you to follow. There are two major outcomes for the seminar. The first allows for student research. By focusing on a specific area within a discipline, the students are able to make a stronger connection with something they enjoy. The second involves presentation skills. Allowing the students to lead the discussion and be responsible for the information and associated materials increases both their understanding and self-efficacy.

Directions for the seminar are as follows:

1. *The Introduction.* Each student must introduce his or her problem or topic by giving a review of the literature—a summary of what already has been written about the topic. Students may start with a short description of the topic concerning the area of their naturalist discipline.

2. *The Fundamentals.* The second aspect of the presentation is to discuss the fundamentals of the topic. This consists of answers to the following questions: What are the interesting facts? Who is involved? What does it tell us? How does it relate to the discipline?

3. *Open Time.* The students can then offer a discussion related to any research ideas they have brainstormed during the preparation of the topic.

4. *Summarize Findings.* Students must make concluding remarks and/or summarize their findings.

5. *Requirements.* Students are to have a handout for the entire class. They can submit a one-page handout to me, and I make the copies for the class. Depending on budget issues, this may not be possible, and so an overhead or poster as a visual aid will suffice.

Students may work as individuals or in small self-selected groups. I have found that some students at this point like to work on their own while others need the support and conversational nature that comes from working in small groups. Individuals and groups are responsible for a 5–10 minute presentation that follows the format discussed above. They must submit a structured outline highlighting all of their individual or group "talking points," as well as a list of references in correct bibliographic format. Quite often, I decide to collect this a week early. It not only allows me to evaluate their research skills, but I am able to organize the presentations in a planned sequence. Presentations should take place in front of the entire class. I have found that this usually takes at least 2 one-hour class periods. If time does not permit this span of time, you could allow a few students or groups to present each day for a week or so. If time is limited, then the groups may have to present to members of their own subcategory of naturalist discipline. It must be noted that the best environment for this is a roundtable discussion, with all students presenting to the entire class.

Following the assigning of the seminar, I do offer the following examples of seminar topic ideas. Students do not have to choose one of these, but they can if they want to. I present them as a way for the students to see the specificity of each of the choices given as examples:

- *Animals:* defense, extinction, migration, habitats
- *Insects:* pheromones, pesticides, plant interactions, invasive vs. native
- *Birds:* distribution, songs, migration routes, wind power's effects on
- *Trees:* old growth forests, deforestation, fungus, rot, protection
- *Plants:* medicinal uses, history of, poisonous, edible
- *Rocks:* sources of fuel, gems, building structures, ground water

I have found it helpful to use the Seminar Information Sheet handout when working with my students. A grading rubric follows.

I have conducted seminars in two types of classroom configurations. I have found that the best classroom configuration for seminars is "in the round." When the classroom consists of tables, I have the students arrange them in a circle so as to increase the seminar experience. In many cases, I have the students speak from their seats. This presents an informal discussion environment separate from an oral presentation. If the students require an easel, projector, or overhead, they are welcome to stand and present.

Having students make oral or written comments and/or questions also can prove quite helpful and supportive in a seminar environment. Remember that one of the goals of a seminar is to create a community of understanding and support. When the students begin to recognize each other's interests and talents, they in turn feel good about their own ideas. Done correctly, a seminar will take time, but be assured it is not time wasted. In my experience, I have found that many ideas for future projects, such as a science fair or a final project, come from these initial supportive environments.

I evaluate the students' seminar with the following criteria:

1. How well they have prepared for the seminar discussion. This comes from their list of references, outline, handout and/or visual aid, and oral discussion.
2. Their response to others' questions/comments.
3. The questions and comments they ask of others.

Shortly after the seminar, I usually begin to post upcoming events related to natural science that are happening in the community. Although I cannot always make time to attend them myself, a simple notice home alerts parents to these events. I dedicate a section of my classroom board where I can pin up different lectures going on in the community. Our local paper has an environmental science section every week that lists lectures, presentations, and demonstrations, which are usually free to the public, and I keep students aware of these events.

I offer you one last piece of advice when organizing a seminar for your students: The more authentic and "real" you can make it, the more the students will feel that their opinions, ideas, and comments are valued.

Seminar Information Sheet

Name(s) _____

_____

Title of Presentation _____

Checklist:

- ❏ Research conducted
- ❏ Information is clear and informative
- ❏ Outline created
- ❏ Images/visual aid (not required)
- ❏ Printed outline
- ❏ Practice

You will have _____ days to research, rehearse, and any make necessary changes. You should be prepared to present on _____. In the event that we cannot get to them all, we will continue each day until complete.

Seminar Information Sheet

Seminar Evaluation Rubric

Name(s) _____

Title of Presentation _____

1. **Research Conducted**   Y   N
    The depth of research can best be described as (circle one)
    ❑ No Stone Unturned
    ❑ Sufficient to Present
    ❑ Slim

2. **Information related to topic**   Y   N
    The information presented can be best described as (circle one)
    ❑ No Stone Unturned
    ❑ Sufficient to Present
    ❑ Slim

3. **Outline created had correct format**   Y   N

4. **Images/visual aid (not required)** Y   N

    If yes, what was the aid? _____
    Image/visual aid can be described as (circle one)
    ❑ Quite Helpful
    ❑ Existent
    ❑ Distracting

Comments: _____

_____

_____

_____

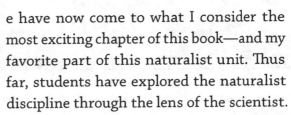

Chapter 6

The Creative Naturalist

We have now come to what I consider the most exciting chapter of this book—and my favorite part of this naturalist unit. Thus far, students have explored the naturalist discipline through the lens of the scientist. Although their observations have sparked wonder and piqued their imaginations, so far their own work has been more or less informational. In this chapter, we examine the naturalist as artist, with the focus on nature poets, writers, artists, and photographers.

Creativity, in all of its manifestations, owes a great deal to the natural world, which is, in itself, inspiring. Throughout history, artists and writers alike have attributed nature with true inspiration, and it is this concept that I try to get across to my students when studying the naturalist discipline. I make it very clear from day one that you need not be a lab scientist or scientific researcher to study nature and its abundance of life and lessons.

> "Only through art can we get outside of ourselves and know another's view of the universe which is not the same as ours and see landscapes which otherwise would have remained unknown to us like the landscapes of the moon."
> —Marcel Proust

Students are excited to learn that naturalists express their observations and love of nature in creative ways.

I carefully explain to the students that many of the greatest naturalists were, and continue to be, writers, artists, photographers, sculptors, inventors, and the like. Not only does this allow the students to be comfortable in studying their chosen field of interest, it strengthens their awareness of the many related disciplines where the naturalist perspective can be found.

The offerings in this chapter also allow for many interdisciplinary connections within your school or community. Language, as well as the performing and visual arts, can be connected to the study of nature. It is a natural fit, no pun intended.

I must make it clear from the onset of this chapter that I am in no way an expert in any of these related fields. What I know has come from my own interest, general study, and appreciation. I, like many of you, have come to appreciate the many facets of art in all of its forms.

Through careful analysis of the resources that exist in these related fields, and in preparation for my own teaching, I have come across a wealth of Web sites and books. I also have developed assignments related to these, which are contained within this chapter.

The Nature Poet

The main goals of this section are not only to expose students to some nature poems and their authors, but also to have them understand the concept of *voice*, which is crucial in many of the disciplines in this chapter. One way to help students understand this concept is to point out that an artist's or writer's voice is tied to his or her individuality—what makes him or her unique. Throughout all of the creative naturalist activities, I constantly refer back to these simple questions:

> "The question is not what you look at, but what you see."
> —Henry David Thoreau

- What is the value of studying nature?
- How does nature inspire art?
- What does it mean to have a "voice"?

I have students read historically significant nature poems, asking that they listen to identify each writer's particular voice. I also have students compare and contrast different nature poems and offer opinions as to the purpose of writing them.

The students in turn use their field books as a means to write a short nature poem expressing their own voice as it relates to what they observed.

I will present in this section some of my favorite nature poems, but, in reality, there are so many choices that such reading lists could (and should) be as unique as each teacher. Picking your own favorites adds a personal touch to the class environment and allows the students a window into your own interests and tastes.

I begin by distributing the following poem. I read it aloud at first and then have the students read it silently.

"A Seed" by William Allingham

See how a Seed, which Autumn flung down,
And through the Winter neglected lay,
Uncoils two little green leaves and two brown,
With tiny root taking hold on the clay
As, lifting and strengthening day by day,
It pushes red branchless, sprouts new leaves,
And cell after cell the Power in it weaves
Out of the storehouse of soil and clime,
To fashion a Tree in due course of time;
Tree with rough bark and boughs' expansion,
Where the Crow can build his mansion,
Or a Man, in some new May,
Lie under whispering leaves and say,
"Are the ills of one's life so very bad
When a Green Tree makes me deliciously glad?"
As I do now. But where shall I be
When this little Seed is a tall green Tree?

When they have completed rereading the poem, pose the following questions:
- What does it mean to have voice in your writing?
- How would you describe Allingham's voice?

My students' spiritedness, coupled with the advanced content in the poem, usually leads to quite an interesting discussion relating not only to the author's voice, but also the "meaning" of the words.

One student invariably suggests that, perhaps, the author was intoxicated and I let him or her know that this conversation is for another day. There actually is a whole study relating to substance abuse and the creative individual, so the student is not far from a research question. Some other off-the-cuff responses I have heard include: "An apple fell on his head," "He is really Johnny Appleseed," and my favorite, "He is too poetic." It is good to allow these kinds of responses, to build upon the strength of your students' free associations in order to steer the conversation into a more serious discussion about artistic voice.

I have taken various approaches with this poem before. The best seems to be to split the class into groups and separate the poem by a group of lines. I then have the students read them silently and then together. I stress that they should try to read it as it was written. If we were looking at the concept of voice in the literal sense then I could have the students stand up and read aloud in the author's voice. Nine times out of ten, the students would give Allingham a British accent.

There are many wonderful texts that offer analysis and criticism of works of poetry. It may help to read up on some literary criticism of any poem you choose to explore with your students—especially if you plan on increasing the depth of the discussion in this area. In the age of the Internet, often a quick search will yield a whole host of criticism on any given poem.

Allingham's poem presents a wealth of possibilities for you to explore. The themes range from birth and death, growing up, being on your own, and challenges and obstacles we face, to the contemplation of life itself. I also have included at the end of this chapter a few more of my favorite nature poems to share with students. Again, you can decide which, if any, to focus on. Feel free to use your own favorites, or to seek out poems you believe will work with your students.

It is a good idea to have students read several poems and then allow them to choose one to analyze. Then, split students into groups: First, group students with those who analyzed the same one, and then group them in a mixed arrangement so that they all hear about the voices of the others.

A good follow-up assignment is to have students seek out a poem on their own and complete an analysis or review, using the skills they learned during the discussion of voice in class. Such an assignment might contain prompts such as:

- Name of the work of poetry,
- Name of the poet,
- Type of poetry (if known),
- How did you hear about or located the work?,
- How would you describe the poet's voice?, and
- What do you think this poet's voice tells you about his or her relationship with the natural world?

Having students study poetry without having them write their own would be a missed opportunity. I always have my students use their field books to write a personal nature poem that expresses their voice, as they now understand it. Their poems will be stemming from real experiences they have had out in the field. Sample instructions might read something like the following:

Using your field notes, you are to write a poem that expresses not only your personal voice, but also what you felt during your observations. It may help if you review some of the poems we have read in class or visit some of the nature poetry Web sites we have visited.

The most important aspect of this, or any lesson in this chapter, is to let the students uncover their own ideas, recognizing the "voice" of the poet, as well as explore their own voice.

Not all of your students will particularly enjoy this medium, nor will they be able to recognize their own voice at the onset of their writing. This should not be looked at as a failure or at all discouraging. Instead of focusing on the negative aspects of their writing, make sure to encourage the positive attributes, urging them to continue. It is through practice and patience that they will uncover their true voice.

The students, having chosen a discipline they are interested in, will find importance in their efforts. Remind them to be themselves and that they should have confidence in what they have to say. Reading their work aloud also will aid in their progress, and the feedback, both positive and negative, will only strengthen their confidence. It is important to make these expectations clear to students before sending them off to write their own poetry.

Teacher Talk

To give an insight into students' "voice," I say, "The most important consideration when writing, composing, or creating something that will be shared with others is the relationship that may or may not exist between the creator and the audience.

"In order for your audience to react to your writing, the use of descriptive words is crucial. When you write using your discovered 'voice,' the narrative feels real, allowing the reader to experience your observations vicariously. Although unlike a conversation or presentation, where eye contact and body language help convey your message, writing can come across in much the same way. The goal in your writing should be to make it believable, authentic, and sincere."

Sample Nature Poems

"Mist" by Henry David Thoreau

Low-anchored cloud,
Newfoundland air,
Fountain head and source of rivers,
Dew-cloth, dream drapery,
And napkin spread by fays;
Drifting meadow of the air,
Where bloom the daisied banks and violets,
And in whose fenny labyrinth
The bittern booms and heron wades;
Spirit of the lake and seas and rivers,
Bear only perfumes and the scent
Of healing herbs to just men's fields!

"A Noiseless, Patient Spider" by Walt Whitman

A NOISELESS, patient spider,
I mark'd, where, on a little promontory, it stood, isolated;
Mark'd how, to explore the vacant, vast surrounding,
It launch'd forth filament, filament, filament, out of itself;
Ever unreeling them—ever tirelessly speeding them.

And you, O my Soul, where you stand,
Surrounded, surrounded, in measureless oceans of space,
Ceaselessly musing, venturing, throwing—seeking the spheres, to con-
nect them;
Till the bridge you will need, be form'd—till the ductile anchor hold;
Till the gossamer thread you fling, catch somewhere, O my Soul.

"The Tree" by Anne Finch

Fair tree! for thy delightful shade
'Tis just that some return be made;
Sure some return is due from me
To thy cool shadows, and to thee.
When thou to birds dost shelter give,
Thou music dost from them receive;
If travellers beneath thee stay
Till storms have worn themselves away,
That time in praising thee they spend
And thy protecting pow'r commend.
The shepherd here, from scorching freed,
Tunes to thy dancing leaves his reed;
Whilst his lov'd nymph, in thanks, bestows
Her flow'ry chaplets on thy boughs.
Shall I then only silent be,
And no return be made by me?
No; let this wish upon thee wait,
And still to flourish be thy fate.
To future ages may'st thou stand
Untouch'd by the rash workman's hand,
Till that large stock of sap is spent,
Which gives thy summer's ornament;
Till the fierce winds, that vainly strive
To shock thy greatness whilst alive,
Shall on thy lifeless hour attend,
Prevent the axe, and grace thy end;
Their scatter'd strength together call
And to the clouds proclaim thy fall;
Who then their ev'ning dews may spare
When thou no longer art their care,
But shalt, like ancient heroes, burn,
And some bright hearth be made thy urn.

Suggested Books

Art & Nature: An Illustrated Anthology of Nature Poetry by Metropolitan Museum of Art & Kate Farrell

Back From the Far Field: American Nature Poetry in the Late Twentieth Century by Bernard W. Quetchenbach

Earth, My Likeness: Nature Poetry of Walt Whitman by Walt Whitman; Howard Nelson (Ed.)

Footprints on the Roof: Poems About the Earth by Marilyn Singer

Glimpses of Nature: Poetry for Children by Victoria Berkhin

Nature: Poems Old and New by May Swenson

Poems for a Small Planet: Contemporary American Nature Poetry edited by Robert Pack and Jay Parini

Poetry for the Earth edited by Sara Dunn and Alan Scholefield

Urban Nature: Poems About Wildlife in the City edited by Laure-Anne Bosselaar

Web Site Resources for Nature Poems

First Science (http://www.firstscience.com/site/poems.asp) features poems inspired by nature and science.

Nature Poetry (http://judithpordon.tripod.com/poetry/id91.html) features inspirational, narrative, and unique poems about nature, animals, trees, flowers, and the weather.

The Nature Essayist

The second lesson related to creativity in nature is designed to expose the students to a variety of nature writers and their essays. It is essential to have them understand and revisit the concept of voice, which is crucial in all of these disciplines, and so a variety of nature essays are distributed to the class.

"My task . . . is, by the power of the written word, to make you hear, to make you feel . . . to make you see."
—Joseph Conrad

Not only will the students read historically significant nature essays in order to understand voice as it is presented through the art form, they also will see the connection between the natural world and their own observations.

> "At best, the genre we call nature writing requires a rare mixture of scientist, philosopher, and poet."
> —Edwin Way Teale in *Green Treasury*

When time is available, I have the students compare and contrast different nature essays, offering opinions as to the purpose of writing them. Students can then use their field books as a means to write a short nature essay expressing their voice as it relates to what they observed.

Of course, I have my favorite nature writers and like to choose a variety of styles and points of view for my students, but you can let your own taste and discretion determine which ones to use. Drawing connections between art forms is a good way to transition between topics.

Teacher Talk

I start off by saying: "Recall that we first discussed the concept of voice in poetry to express feelings about nature. Today we will look at some nature writers who use the essay as their way of expressing voice. You will find that there are many different ways of writing about nature."

I encourage the students to express themselves by using the observations they have made, the feelings that they have, and the points they wish to get across. It is helpful to stress to your students to look for the interconnectedness and interrelationships among what they observe in nature—between animals and plants, plants and environment, man and nature, and so on.

In introducing the nature essay to students, I find a short reading from any of the following works to be exemplary: *Nature* by Ralph Waldo Emerson, *The Immense Journey* or *The Star Thrower* by Loren Eiseley, *Rising From the Plains* by John McFee,

Naturalist by E. O. Wilson, *Silent Spring* or *The Sea Around Us* by Rachel Carson, and *Walking* or *Walden* by Henry David Thoreau.

I also suggest the following chapters and essays for consideration in your classroom, but feel free to choose whichever you like. I find that assigning readings from the introductions to the texts work very well for the students, allowing them to grasp an understanding for the book.

- "The Slit," "The Flow of the River," "The Star Thrower," and "How Flowers Changed the World" are great selections by Loren Eiseley.
- The first chapter of *Naturalist* by E. O. Wilson is outstanding.
- "Walking," "Autumnal Tints," and "Huckleberries" by Henry David Thoreau are great to use.
- Anything by Rachel Carson is incredible.
- John McFee's *The Control of Nature* is great for those interested in geology and history.

Short, punchy quotes are also an excellent way to introduce the beauty of nature prose. I often begin by sharing the following quotes with the students to introduce them to the writings and style of each of the authors.

"The more clearly we can focus our attention on the wonders and realities of the universe about us, the less taste we shall have for destruction."

—Rachel Carson

"Though we travel the world over to find the beautiful, we must carry it with us or we find it not."

—Ralph Waldo Emerson

"It is the natural history that led Hudson to glimpse eternity in some old men's faces at Land's End, that led Thoreau to see human civilizations as toadstools sprung up in the night by solitary roads, or that provoked Melville to experience in the sight of a sperm whale some colossal alien existence without which man himself would be incomplete."

—Loren Eiseley

"Most children have a bug period. I never grew out of mine."

—E. O. Wilson

"Nature is full of genius, full of the divinity; so that not a snowflake escapes its fashioning hand."

—Henry David Thoreau

Teachers can assign questions based on the readings of their choice. I advise teachers to allow for times of reflection during this time.

If more time is available, I put the children into reading groups. They could read sample essays or even entire texts. It should be noted that some texts present more challenging reading levels than others. This serves well in differentiating in the classroom.

A reading cube (see Figure 6) could serve as a way to generate ideas at the onset. It also could be used when reading the poetry discussed earlier. Simply create six text boxes with questions, cut out, fold, and tape. It provides an exciting activity to introduce the questions and can be used with the full class or in groups.

More Suggested Nature Essays and Books

American Nature Writers edited by John Elder

The Best American Science and Nature Writing (The Best American Series) edited by Brian Greene

The Best Nature Writing of Joseph Wood Krutch by Joseph Wood Krutch

Coming Into the Country by John McPhee

Desert Solitaire: A Season in the Wilderness by Edward Abbey

The Edge of the Sea by Rachel Carson

John Burroughs' America: Selections From the Writings of the Hudson River Naturalist by John Burroughs; Farida Wiley (Ed.)

The Illustrated Walden by Henry David Thoreau

Lost Woods: The Discovered Writing of Rachel Carson edited by Linda Lear

The Norton Book of Nature Writing edited by Robert Finch and John Elder

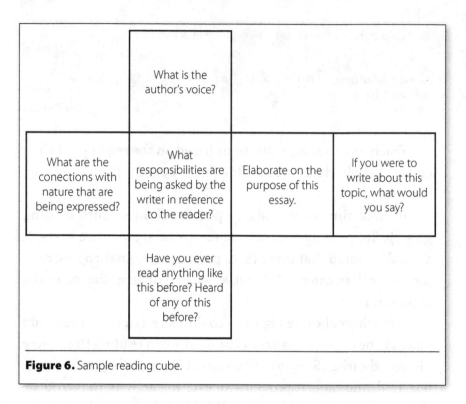

Figure 6. Sample reading cube.

A Sand County Almanac and Sketches Here and There by Aldo Leopold

The Solace of Open Spaces by Gretel Ehrlich

Wild America: The Record of a 30,000-Mile Journey Around the Continent by a Distinguished Naturalist and his British Colleague by Roger Tory Peterson and James Fisher

Web Sites for Nature Writers

Abbey's Web (http://www.abbeyweb.net/abbey.html) contains articles about Edward Abbey, introductory and biographical information, a bibliography, quotes, and links.

Robert Winkler's Web Page (http://pages.cthome.net/rwinkler/index.htm) showcases this excellent nature writer and provides a wealth of resources.

The Sierra Club's John Muir Exhibit (http://www.sierraclub.org/john_muir_exhibit) contains excerpts of selected Muir books and articles.

The Thoreau Reader (http://thoreau.eserver.org) contains three complete
    books and four essays by Thoreau.

Transcendentalists.com (http://www.transcendentalists.com/1emerson.
    html) has a great collection of links on Ralph Waldo Emerson and on
    the American Transcendentalism movement.

The Walden Woods Project (http://www.walden.org) contains information
    on education, research, and activism related to conservation.

All I Need Is a Canvas:
The Nature Artist and Nature Photographer

This final section seeks to expose students to a variety of
nature artists and their works and also to have them understand
the concept of design and revisit the concept of
voice.

> "To the artist there is never anything ugly in nature."
> —Auguste Rodin

I have the students view historically significant
art in order to understand voice and interpretation
as it is presented through the art form. It is helpful to explain
that a visual artist's "voice" encompasses the same inner dimen-
sions as the writer. Both have ideas and emotions they wish to
express; it is only the medium that differs.

Students can use their field books as a means to write ideas
for their own artwork and, if there is an art teacher who can be
utilized, a more in-depth discussion and application can take
place. Not only do I use the Web and books as resources, I also
generally take my class to a museum to view works firsthand.
However, whether students view art in person, in a book, or on
a screen, the assignment included in this chapter will test their
observational and communication skills.

For this section, I usually choose to use four nature artists.
Again, feel free to allow your own taste and knowledge to inform
your selections. Some of my favorites, and those with whom I've

had success with students, include Ansel Adams, Edward Weston, Georgia O'Keeffe, and Albert Bierstadt.

Teacher Talk

To introduce this new section, I say, "Today we are going to look at another art form, visual photographs and artwork. I will be dividing you into four groups. You are to read about the artist using the biographies provided and discuss his or her voice as you see it through the artwork. Try to imagine that you are the artist. What are the motivating factors for you to complete the work? How do you feel? If you would like to, rename the piece."

It would be helpful to do some background research on each artist and have some large images for the students to view. I also provide short biographies on each artist as well, in order that the students may come to know them better.

Some basic definition of terms should follow. Although it may be review for some students, all should be made familiar with a sample of different artistic media (oil and watercolor paint, photography, clay, stone, and so on). A short, introductory discussion about art appreciation and criticism is usually in order. Although students should be reassured that their instinctual, visceral responses to art are as valid as that of any critic, they should be encouraged to bring to bear the same observational skills they use in the field on a piece of art. Much like nature, appreciation of art is only enhanced by close observation and understanding. To guide students in their observations, I usually provide a handout similar to the one found at the end of the chapter.

To allow students to further synthesize what they have observed and learned from a piece of art, I often have them write an art review. Using the notes and observations they recorded on the Critical Observation of Art handout, students will then follow the directions on the Art Review handout on the next page to craft a written review. This process would be the same whether students have observed a work of art in person during a trip to a museum, in a book, or online.

Suggested Nature Photography Books

The Art of Photographing Nature by Martha Hill

Essential Skills for Nature Photography by Cub Kahn

The Magic of Digital Nature Photography by Rob Sheppard

The Nature of America: Images by North America's Premiere Nature Photographers by David Middleton and Bill Fortney

John Shaw's Closeups in Nature by John Shaw

John Shaw's Nature Photography Field Guide by John Shaw

Nature Photography Web Sites

North American Nature Photography Association (http://www.nanpa.org) is the first and only association in North America committed solely to serving the field of nature photography.

Nature Photographer Magazine (http://www.naturephotographermag.com) features amazing spreads from some of the greatest eyes in nature photography.

Nature Photographers Network (http://www.naturephotographers.net) features an online magazine and the official site of the Nature Photographers Network.

Suggested Nature Art Books

Albert Bierstadt by Gordon Hendricks

Andy Goldsworthy: A Collaboration With Nature by Andy Goldsworthy

Artist's Photo Reference: Landscapes by Gary Greene

Creating Nature in Watercolor: An Artist's Guide by Cathy Johnson

Georgia O'Keeffe: Nature and Abstraction by Richard D. Marshall, Achille Bonito Oliva, and Yvonne Scott

Nature Artists Web Sites

The Ansel Adams Gallery (http://www.anseladams.com) has been owned and operated by the Ansel Adams family since its founding as a painter's studio in 1902. The site contains a wonderful collection of Adams' nature photography.

Artists for Conservation (http://www.natureartists.com) presents a wealth of nature artists from across the globe.

Edward Weston's Web site (http://www.edward-weston.com) contains information about and works by one of the most influential American photographers of the 20th century.

The Georgia O'Keefe Museum (http://www.okeeffemuseum.org) is steward to more than half of O'Keeffe's artwork. The museum displays her work in some of the galleries on a rotating basis throughout the year, and the site contains wonderful galleries and slideshows of her work.

White Mountain Art & Artists (http://whitemountainart.com) contains a collection of biographies and works by Northeastern American artists, including a great collection of Albert Bierstadt's landscapes.

Critical Observation of Art

Name of Artist _____

Name of Work _____

Medium (oil paint, clay, photograph, etc.) _____

Describe the Work

What kinds of things do you see in this artwork? Be specific. _____

_____

_____

_____

What words would you use to describe this painting? What other words might we use?

_____

_____

_____

How would you describe the lines in this artwork? Are they smooth? Rough? Describe the shapes, angles, and colors.

_____

_____

_____

How would you describe this artwork to a person who could not see it?

_____

_____

_____

Critical Observation of Art

Relate the Work

What does this artwork remind you of? _____

_____

_____

_____

What things do you recognize in this artwork? What things seem new to you?

_____

_____

_____

What interests you most about this work of art?

_____

_____

_____

Analyze the Work

What do you think is the most important part of this artwork? _____

_____

_____

_____

How do you think the artist made this work? _____

_____

_____

_____

What questions would you ask the artist about this work if he or she were here?

_____

_____

_____

Critical Observation of Art

Interpret the Work

What title would you give to this artwork? What made you decide on that title?

_____

_____

_____

What do you think this artwork is about? How did you come up that idea?

_____

_____

_____

Why do you suppose the artist made this artwork? What do you think inspired the artist?

_____

_____

_____

Evaluate the Work

What do you see as the strenghts of the artwork? What do you see as the weaknesses?

_____

_____

_____

What would you do with this work if you owned it?

_____

_____

_____

What do you think is worth remembering about this artwork?

_____

_____

_____

Critical Observation of Art

Art Review

Directions

Imagine you are an art critic writing for an audience of fellow art lovers. Using the notes and observations you made on the Critical Observation of Art handout, you will write a review of the piece of artwork that you studied. Your review must include the information listed below and be typed and double-spaced. Attach the Critical Observation of Art handout to your review.

- Name of the piece of art
- Name of the artist
- Medium (e.g., oil or watercolor paint, photograph, sculpture, and so on)
- Location/gallery
- Address at least one question from each of the categories from the Critical Observation of Art handout (Describe, Relate, Analyze, Interpret, Evaluate). A good organizational tip is to first highlight the questions on the observation handout that you will address in your review.

Chapter 7
Researchers at Work

I have found that many of my students actually enjoy seeing the real-world scientific applications of fieldwork. Although many of them choose to explore a creative outlet for the final project, it is necessary to stress that many naturalists aid in and conduct research on a variety of topics in their discipline areas. This chapter is not meant to instruct about the process for conducting research and writing research papers, as there are many texts that already do a fine job in this area. A list of these resources can be found at the end of the chapter. What I offer are some discussion questions and ideas for resources that will serve to illuminate for students the purpose and some of the norms of research in naturalist fields. Finally, this lesson will ultimately empower students in their final independent project, whether they decide to pursue a traditional research paper or a more creative outlet for their findings.

The students first are introduced to what a professional research paper looks like and are shown table of contents from scholarly journals in their fields. They then are placed into groups based on

"When nature has work to be done, she creates a genius to do it."
—Ralph Waldo Emerson

their discipline and given a selection of research papers from their respective fields. They read and discuss the articles in order to complete a Research Paper Analysis handout, which you will find near the end of the chapter.

It is important to keep in mind that the students should still try to uncover the author's or authors' voice. In the area of research, it is great to make the connection between genres of writing and art styles. The students will see that although the authors possess a voice of their own, there is often a prescriptive formula for conducting the research and offering data and results.

Teacher Talk

To introduce this topic, I say, "Hello class, I know we have done a lot in such a short time, and I am sure you are eager to return to some authentic fieldwork. We will soon be returning to the outdoors to complete our naturalistic observations, as you will be using them to complete a final project for this unit. Before we do that, however, I would like for you to look at another way that naturalists convey what they have observed. In this case, it is in the form of a research paper. It is through these important research papers that scientists are able to make a difference in the world, influence policy, and educate people."

Here are some questions that may be useful in analyzing various kinds of research papers. I create a worksheet from these questions that I distribute to the groups of students, including:
- What is the overall purpose of the research?
- How does the research fit into the context of its field?
- What are the major findings of the study? (Look in the Abstract and Conclusion.)
- What further experiments can you think of to continue the research or to answer remaining questions?

I usually acquire the research papers by a few means. Many professional papers, some outdated but great to use for this purpose, are available online through a search using Google Scholar. I also have a collection of research journals that I have amassed over time. A trip to a college library would be the best environment for this lesson. Depending on the age group of the students, teaching them to use a database or journal search engines might be timely. An adaptation of this lesson for your students might be to look at articles found in magazines such as *National Geographic, Earth,* or *Discover.* Although these are not strict in terms of research methodology, they do follow a format for students to analyze.

Some things to keep in mind:

1. Consider the reading ease or difficulty of the selected works. Although this is not the primary concern, some vocabulary and content is extremely difficult to understand, even for the trained professional, seasoned educator, and advanced student.

2. It is a good idea to give each student his or her own copy of the paper or article.

3. I have found that connecting this work to their own fieldwork and seminar presentations strengthens their understanding of the topic and selection, so finding articles that directly relate is quite helpful.

4. The students can think back to their exploration of naturalist societies and see what journals they publish. It is a great place to start.

5. I usually make use of the references section in research journals, instructing the students on their purpose as research tools themselves.

6. It is a good idea during this time for you to allow students to formulate their own research questions and ideas for

the title of a research paper that they might like to write. Although this may or may not be used at a later date, it serves as a way to get them thinking.

Once the instructions have been given and groups are selected, papers can be distributed along with the Research Paper Analysis worksheet. The groups will fill in the form and choose a presenter from the group present the findings to the class.

Suggested Books

How to Write and Publish a Scientific Paper by Robert S. Day

A Field Guide for Science Writers edited by Deborah Blum, Mary Knudson, and Robin Marantz Henig

Preparing Scientific Illustrations: A Guide to Better Posters, Presentations, and Publications by Mary Helen Briscoe

Scientific Papers and Presentations by Martha Davis

Research Paper Analysis

Name of research paper and topic of interest: _____

_____

Abstract or summary of paper: _____

_____

_____

_____

What was the hypothesis, goal, or assumption that was stated?

_____

_____

_____

How were results gathered and what were the results? What tools were used?

_____

_____

_____

What did the author(s) conclude from the results?

_____

_____

_____

Describe any interesting ideas or facts.

_____

_____

_____

Research Paper Analysis

Chapter 8

Putting It All Together:
The Final Project

There perhaps is nothing more personally gratifying than witnessing firsthand the application of newly acquired knowledge by the students. I often am surprised to hear students say, "This is easy," when in reality they have worked so hard to attain the skills needed for an independent project such as the one to be discussed in this chapter. I need to remind them that they do not give themselves the credit they deserve and that instead of saying the work is easy, they should be proud of all they have learned and accomplished.

This chapter includes the assignment for the final project and the accompanying assessment I use. Only you can judge when your students are ready to begin this final work. As you will see, there is great choice and variety in terms of the naturalist area chosen, the medium for the product, and the audience for which it will be presented. As with all other choices and assignments, the work must come from the heart of the student. The students,

"Knowledge is of two kinds. We know a subject ourselves, or we know where we can find information on it."
— Samuel Johnson

"Science may set limits to knowledge, but should not set limits to imagination."
—Bertrand Russell

who have taken on the role of zoologist, geologist, biologist, botanist, or entomologist, will now become the researcher, the writer, the painter, the photographer, the essayist, the poet—the *naturalist*. Individual assessment will be based upon the student's field notes, level of displayed effort, conveyance of voice, strength of research, and documentation of process.

At its heart, the assignment involves all of the skills learned throughout the unit of instruction. However, student success hinges on the allotment of outdoor fieldwork that will serve as the preparation for the project. This, coupled with the student's creativity, has the potential to yield some pretty amazing work. A couple of examples of final projects from my students include an activity book on five common animals in our state and an excellent photographic essay (see Figures 7 and 8). With the right preparation and planning, there is no limit to what your students can achieve.

By way of introducing the final project, it helps to make sure your students understand that they have been working toward this moment since the beginning of the unit.

Teacher Talk

I say, "Today is the day you are going to get your final project assignment. You will be using all of the skills and knowledge you have acquired as you explore a specific area in the natural world, document your findings in your field books, research your topic, and create a product that you will present your findings to an audience. You will have the choice as to what your final product will be. Your final project will be completed in a series of steps that I will outline for you. You are to have each one checked off before you begin the next step."

Figure 7. Sample final project: Student-created activity book on common mammals of Rhode Island.

Figure 8. Sample final project: Student photograph of a lobster.

After this short introduction, I distribute a copy of the checklist sheet, assignment form, and grading rubric, all of which you will find at the end of this chapter.

I choose to have the students work on this project independently, and so I only check on them periodically, making sure that they are progressing and keeping to deadlines they have set for themselves. Students will choose an audience to which they will target their final projects, and I have found this works best when students actually present their projects to this audience. Students become more vested in their work knowing someone other than their teacher will be evaluating it. Of course, you may choose to have students simply present to the class.

The final project checklist contains the following items that I have annotated below:

1. *Naturalist Project Graphic Organizer filled in and complete:* Students must complete their graphic organizer, which is given to them at the start of the unit (see Figure 2 in Chapter 1). I usually collect these periodically or review them when the students are conducting in-class projects.

2. *Field notes complete:* Their field notes must be neat, organized, and turned in with their final work. Careful attention is paid to past rubrics dealing with the individual student's progress in completing field notes.

3. *Resources gathered and list handed in:* If their project requires research, a complete and correct bibliographic list should be shared with you before students begin writing.

4. *Audience sought out:* Students must make a connection with their audience. This may be in the form of an e-mail, phone call, or contest entry. The goal is to have their work displayed, published, or used in some way. I often take a class period or portion of class time to exploring the

local yellow pages or online communities. Student need is evaluated on a case-by-case basis, as some students have a more outgoing nature than others. I've often helped students make the first contact with potential audiences.

5. *How-to book or methodological skill understood:* Perhaps your students are writing an editorial, nature essay, or journal article; displaying their work at a studio; or creating a PowerPoint presentation or pamphlet. They may need to seek out a "how-to" book or other resources to help them along. I usually help the students locate resources and perhaps even find them a mentor. Oftentimes, this portion is not a requirement for all students. Simple consultations with a student can help in deciding who should access additional resources.

6. *Abstract of product written up and checked off:* I need to have an idea of their project plan, so I instruct students to let me know ahead of time. I set a deadline for abstracts, usually a week after the project is assigned. This three or four sentence explanation of the project helps me approve the plan or work with the student to develop it further. It is a requirement to have this abstract approved.

7. *Final product complete and turned in:* The final product is finished and has been submitted to the teacher.

8. *Evaluation rubric complete:* The rubric addresses the five major objectives of the final project: methodological skills, connection with nature, sense of personal voice, product completion, and audience location and acceptance. The teacher should fill out the rubric for students. Quite often, although not required, the students develop a personalized evaluation for their audience members to complete. These could be filled out by students, other teachers, parents, and the like. One student even received

a stack of thank-you letters from an entire classroom of fourth graders.

9. *Presented to audience:* The students must arrange for their work to be displayed or presented, possibly published, or entered into a contest. In some cases, a class presentation is sufficient. Some students may not be ready to present to an outside audience and need to practice before a more familiar audience at first.

I create individual checklists based on the previous list and have the students set deadlines for when some of these benchmarks will be met. I have found that the addition of planning calendars help as well, although some students need more organizational help than others.

The assessment rubric (see pp. 104–105) contains the categories we have used in all of the previous rubrics: *backyard naturalist, student naturalist, university naturalist,* and *expert in the field.* I have found that using these, instead of the common "excellent," "good," etc., work better, ensuring that all students feel a sense of success. They then are rated on a four-point scale for each of the following objectives:

- methodological skills,
- connection with nature,
- sense of personal voice,
- product completion, and
- audience location and acceptance.

Assessment: Narrative Report Card

In order to substantially evaluate each student's individual performance throughout the entire unit of instruction, I choose to use a written narrative in place of a traditional report card. Not only does this allow me to focus on strengths and weaknesses for each student when commenting on skills and understandings, but it also allows for the personalization of each individual report. Obviously, different schools have different policies, and most schools still use traditional letter- or number-graded report cards. If this is the case in your school, I urge you to supplement such reports with a narrative report, especially during a unit where performance is difficult to quantify, such as this. Providing this valid feedback presents great value for both students and parents, and although it may be time consuming to go into the depth illustrated in the sample narratives, a simple written comment at the end of the evaluation rubric can make all the difference.

The first task is to write a description of the material covered over the course of the term, highlighting all of the major lessons and assignments. The following example contains the assignments as presented in this book.

Description of Material Covered in Unit

The first trimester focused on the natural history unit and sought to expose the students to the concept as it related to the field of natural science. The curriculum presented an attempt to return to the roots of science education. By allowing students to pursue an interest in the natural world, focusing on the methodologies needed to conduct fieldwork, enabling them to see and ponder the connections they perceive, and embarking upon a problem-solving approach to some naturalistic issue in their own neighborhoods, the goal was to awaken these young naturalists, allowing them to understand and be aware of their attachment to the natural world.

The unit began with several lessons focused on the methodological skills of a naturalist. Students were allowed to choose a scientific discipline, recognize its title, and explore questions one would ask, tasks one would accomplish, and tools one would use if one were an expert in the field. Students researched varieties of species and/or types common to our state and returned ready to create a fact sheet using newly learned desktop publishing skills. The students were issued professional field books and were asked to make regular observations and sketches as assigned. The students also studied the naturalist tradition from its roots. They read parts of text, created outlines, and organized oral presentations for the class. They visited a natural history museum, conducted observations there, and participated in a field trip where naturalist investigations were conducted.

Students were then introduced to the concept of "voice" and participated in a variety of activities that reinforced this idea. Students read the words of nature poets, columnists, and essayists; viewed the work of nature photographers and artists; and examined examples of journal articles from the scientific community. In an effort for them to develop their own personal voice, they used expository writing to express their opinions, feelings, and beliefs related to nature.

Students organized small-group seminars dealing with a specific topic related to their field of choice. They further refined their public speaking skills while enriching their understanding of the topics at hand.

Students then began work on their final project. Equipped with the methodological and general skills taught to them, knowledge of where to locate sources of information, and opinions to share with others, students were asked to present their ideas in one of a variety of formats. Student assessment was based upon the field notes, level of displayed effort, conveyance of voice, strength of research, and documentation of process.

Sample Narrative Assessments

Assessing each student presents a unique situation, so below you will find examples from both ends of the achievement spectrum. What follows is a sample report for a student who has mastered the skills throughout the unit.

> Joan has worked very hard during the trimester. I am happy to see such a dedicated and committed student. This is evident not only in her daily work, but during class participation, group assignments, and field efforts. She took on the role of botanist with ease, asking relevant questions and seeking to understand the nature of the field. I was impressed by her seminar presentation dealing with poisonous plants. The class learned a lot, and it was clear that she planned well for the talk. I am eagerly anticipating the evaluation of her final project. Her choice of a children's book is perfect for her to display her skills as a naturalist and convey those to a younger audience. I commend Joan on her work thus far and I encourage her to keep it up. Great job this term, Joan!
>
> In terms of methodological skills, her field notes were of high quality, demonstrating correct skills and offering correct labels, detail, and careful analysis of field studies. Joan was able to make a connection with nature, offering substantial answers to essential questions and recognizing advanced principles. Joan's writing and sharing of opinions offered a strong and genuine sense of personal voice. It was clear that she had something

to say. Joan went above and beyond what was asked of her in her long- and short-term projects. She was quite diligent in completing them. She followed instructions, completed everything on time, and demonstrated a high amount of creativity and effort. Joan's oral presentation skills proved to be good, but I had some suggestions for improvement in areas of organization and presentation. Her retention and demonstration of skills acquisition was exemplary during this first term. I urge her to keep this high level of effort and diligence throughout the year.

Below is an assessment for a student requiring more effort, diligence, and attention.

Charlie had a good term. There has been an uphill trend as it relates to his work throughout the entire term. Charlie started off the year by turning in minimal work, and seemed to let his excitement get the best of him. Upon becoming comfortable in his role as a botanist, Charlie's talents began to shine. He began to formulate thoughtful questions, consulted me before and after class, and also participated during class discussions. Although his humor still sometimes gets the better of him, it is clear that he is working hard to channel his excess energy. His seminar presentation that focused on medicinal uses of plants not only demonstrated planning and organization, but was also well received by the class. I commend him on his efforts and I look forward to evaluating Charlie's final project. I know he has been working hard at it.

In terms of methodological skills, Charlie's field notes were of acceptable quality, although labels, sketches, and details were often missing. Charlie began to grasp a connection with nature and briefly touched upon the basic principles and essential questions. Charlie's writing and sharing of opinions offered a good insight into his sense of personal voice. It was clear that he had something to say, and I have encouraged him to explore further. Charlie was quite diligent in completing his long- and short-term projects. He followed instructions, completed everything on time, and demonstrated a high amount of creativity and effort. Charlie's oral presentation skills proved to be good, but I had some suggestions for improvement in areas of organization and presentation. His retention and demonstration of skills acquisition was sufficient during this first term. I urge him to work a little harder in terms of effort and diligence throughout the year.

The use of the written narrative will open up a dialogue for yourself and your students. They will see themselves as individuals in your eyes. I consistently stress the idea that there is always something to work on. We all have areas in which we excel and areas we can improve. Once the students' eyes are open to that idea, they become more relaxed and accustomed to the classroom situation.

The final project has proven to be quite effective in solidifying the skills taught to the students during the allotted time. It is the most exciting part of the year for me. In years past, I have had students display their work at local coffee shops, studios, and libraries. They have taught lessons to local grammar schools. Some have even created pamphlets for the local zoo and children's museum. Students have entered photo and writing contests, written children's books, and submitted essays and editorials to local and regional papers.

By allowing your students to pursue an area of interest, you will receive better work, observe motivation and excitement, and create an atmosphere of creativity and ease. If time permits, I often include a lesson explaining how to go about contacting the local media and accessing other resources. Like any other lessons taught, the first time around will present a challenge, but as the years go by, and projects accumulate, the students before you will strive to higher standards. It will not only be rewarding for them, but rewarding for you as well.

Final Project Checklist

Student Name _____

1. Naturalist Project Graphic Organizer filled in and complete   _____ date

2. Field notes complete   _____ date

3. Resources gathered and list handed in   _____ date

4. Audience sought out   _____ date

5. How-to book acquired or methodological skill understood   _____ date

6. Abstract of product written up and checked off   _____ date

7. Final product complete and turned in   _____ date

8. Evaluation rubric complete   _____ date

9. Presented to audience   _____ date

Final Project Assignment: "I Am a Naturalist"

Introduction
It is now time to demonstrate your skills as a naturalist, find your "voice," and share some knowledge with your peers through a medium of your choosing. Be sure to read all of the directions to be certain that each part of your project is complete.

Part 1: Selection of a Role
This part relates directly to your naturalist discipline. Which best describes you?
- Biologist
- Botanist
- Ecologist
- Entomologist
- Geologist
- Zoologist
- Other (specify) _____

Part 2: Selection of a Format
This part relates to how you will present your findings, share your personal voice, and seek to educate your audience. Format choices include the following:
- *Photographic Collection.* This collection will display a study of the natural environment and will be completed with accompanying one-paragraph explanations and/or a one-page description of the collection. There are to be a minimum of four photographs and each must be 8" by 10" in size, black-and-white or color.
- *Nature Essay.* Writing in the style of the essayists discussed in class, you are to use your findings to reflect upon an aspect of nature. Think of the inter-relationships you see, the principles that are expressed, and the personal and cultural messages you wish to express. The essay must be a minimum length of four pages, double-spaced, 12-point font.
- *Poetry Collection.* Writing in the style of past and present poets, you are to use your findings to reflect upon an aspect of nature. Think of the inter-relationships you see, the principles that are expressed, and the personal and cultural message you wish to convey. The collection must include a minimum of eight poems of no less than 10 lines each, and it must be bound in a creative manner.

- *Research Paper.* This paper should be written in journal-style format, complete with a list of references. You are to look at an area of nature and pose a question or hypothesis. You may start simple, such as with a complete survey of a specific species or rock type, or you may go into depth by posing a more advanced question. This paper is to include photos of samples from the field, data, and observations, and must have a conclusion. The paper must be a minimum length of four pages, double-spaced, 12-point font. Use at least four sources. Correct bibliographic format is required.
- *Collection of Artwork.* This collection will display a study of the natural environment and will be completed with accompanying one-paragraph explanations and/or a one-page description of the collection of artwork. There is to be a minimum of four art pieces; they can be oil, acrylic, watercolor, pen and ink, or pencil. Each is to be mounted.
- *Newspaper Editorial.* Writing in the style of current editorial writers, you are to use your findings to reflect upon an aspect of nature. Think of the interrelationships you see, the principles that are expressed, and the personal and cultural messages you wish to put across to your readers. Your piece should aim to persuade your audience to share your opinion. The editorial must be a minimum length of two pages, double-spaced, 12-point font.
- *Pamphlet or PowerPoint Presentation.* You may wish to present your findings in a medium that could be presented to a wider audience. Remember that the goal of a presented work is to educate or persuade. Consider an area you wish people to visit, what they will observe when they get there, and ideas about the location's significance you want to share. This could be a local park, preserve, or sanctuary. It may be your own backyard. The audience may be your own friends and family or may be a local library group, park, zoo, or nature preserve. Pamphlet must be tri-folded, or PowerPoint must be a minimum of 10 slides.
- *Lesson Plan for a Classroom.* You may wish to organize your findings into a classroom lesson plan. This could include stories, activities, demonstrations, and the like. You are to type your lesson plan and include time needed for each activity. You also must arrange for your lesson to be used in a classroom of appropriate age. It would help if you had an exit survey of the students you taught to see if you met your lesson objectives.
- *The American Museum of Natural History Young Naturalist Awards.* This is a contest sponsored by the museum. It posts a topic each year and offers a chance for students to be recognized. The judging criteria, rules, entry forms, and help are available online at http://www.amnh.org/nationalcenter/youngnaturalistawards. There also are sample ideas from past entries and lists of winners available to you.

- *Other Idea.* Feel free to present a choice to me. In the past, students have created sculptures, combined some of the above selections, and written and illustrated a children's book, scrapbook, or book of children's activities.

Part 3: Selection of an Audience

You will share your project with a specific audience. It may be a field of experts, people who are interested in your topic, or another audience of your choosing. Examples include:
- newspaper readers,
- zoo patrons,
- society members,
- students,
- judges for contests,
- art studio show patrons, and
- neighborhood groups.

Part 4: Selection of a Topic

This is an endless list, and perhaps you wish to think of one on your own. Here are some sample topics others have chosen in the past:
- how a zoo recreates the natural environments for its animals,
- how invasive crab species appear on the shorelines,
- the glacial and bedrock geological features of the area surrounding our school,
- common medicinal plants found in our state,
- the changing population levels of the birds of our state, and
- a comparison study of leaf litter analysis in rural and urban areas.

Final Project Assignment: "I Am a Naturalist"

Naturalist Project Grading Rubric

Objectives	Backyard Naturalist	Student Naturalist	University Naturalist	Expert in the Field	Earned Points
Methodological Skills: • Displays correct format in field notes • Field notes are organized • Field notes are correctly labeled, containing sketches and relevant information	**1 point** Your field notes were sloppily done, missing labels, detail, and sketches. There was little effort visible.	**2 points** Your field notes were of acceptable quality, although labels, sketches, and detail often were missing.	**3 points** Your field notes were of high quality, demonstrating correct skills and labels, detailed field notes, and careful analysis of field studies.	**4 points** Your field notes were of expert quality, demonstrating correct skills and labels, detailed field notes, and careful analysis of field studies. Notes went above and beyond requirements.	
Connection With Nature: • Understandings and essential questions are addressed • Product displays sense of connection with nature	**1 point** You made little connection with nature. Principles and essential questions were not addressed.	**2 points** You began to grasp a connection with nature and briefly touched upon the basic principles and essential questions.	**3 points** You were able to make a connection with nature, offering substantial answers to essential questions and recognizing advanced principles.	**4 points** You were able to make a strong connection with nature, offering substantial answers to essential questions and recognizing advanced principles in a way that was outmatched.	
Sense of Personal Voice: • Student understands voice • Student was able to find his or her voice • Voice was evident • Voice was unique and genuine	**1 point** You showed little evidence of seeking a personal voice.	**2 points** You began to show some understanding of what it means to have a personal voice. Explore further and you will find one unique to you.	**3 points** You have found your voice and it is genuine. It was clear that you had something to say and you did in your own way.	**4 points** You have found your voice and it is true and genuine. It is clear that you have something to say and can articulate it very well.	

Naturalist Project Grading Rubric

Naturalist Project Grading Rubric

Objectives	Backyard Naturalist	Student Naturalist	University Naturalist	Expert in the Field	Earned Points
Product Completion: • Directions and outline were followed • Regular consultations were made between teacher and student • Work was completed with a high amount of creativity, task commitment, and ability	**1 point** You made little effort to follow directions and as a result did not complete your project.	**2 points** You did make some effort to complete your project, but more consultations and effort would have aided in the completion of the project and its quality.	**3 points** You were quite diligent in completing your project. You followed instructions, completed tasks on time, and demonstrated a high amount of effort and creativity.	**4 points** You have gone above and beyond what was asked. You were quite diligent in completing your project. You followed instructions, completed tasks on time, and demonstrated a high amount of effort and creativity.	
Audience Location and Acceptance: • Audience was located • Audience was contacted • Presentation planned • Audience acceptance and evaluation	**1 point** You were unsuccessful in finding or contacting an audience, and as a result, could not present.	**2 points** You were successful in locating your audience and, while you did contact them, did not present.	**3 points** You were successful in locating, contacting, and presenting to your target audience. It was a great match.	**4 points** You were successful in locating, contacting, and presenting to your target audience. It was a great match. Your work was of a quality that it could be published or accepted as professional work.	
				Score:	

Chapter 9

Extending and Localizing the Unit:

Activities for Teachers and Students

One of the beauties of studying the fields of nature and natural history is that the resources available are virtually endless. Nature surrounds us, envelopes us, and no matter where we look, we can find something to relate back to the natural world. In my search to provide the best resources for my students, I have amassed a strong set of core ones that I consider to be the best, and these can found at the end of each chapter. There is no rhyme or reason for leaving out the many other excellent ones that exist. Only know that as you begin your search for supplementary materials, you will have your favorites too.

> "Choose only one master—Nature."
> —Rembrandt

Supplementing and Supporting Instruction With a Web Site

Nearly all of the resources discussed in this book are accessible through the Internet. For my classes, I have designed a Web site that makes use of the lessons, forms, resources, and Web sites found throughout each chapter. Not only does it help organize information for myself as the educator, but it also has allowed my students to access the information from remote locations. Parents are greatly impressed and excited to know that the curriculum and resources are presented in this format. This also has proven quite helpful in terms of homework as well as long- and short-term assignments. Figure 9 is a screenshot from the Web site I currently use in the classroom.

I use several images on my landing page, which is the page students see first when they visit the site. Visitors are then directed to the Table of Contents section, where they can link to the introduction to the unit, a note from me, as well as an overview of the unit. There also is a link for handouts. I post anything here that I hand out in class. These may be forms to fill out or homework assignments. I also include links, organized by discipline, related to natural history in Rhode Island (my home state) that I have researched and posted for student use. This serves as a good starting-off point for the students in their research. You could do the same with Web sites pertaining to your own region. I conclude with a page where I post other sites of interests, contests, and species-identification resources.

Among the most useful items on the Web site are my lesson plans. Parents and students alike find it helpful to access the lessons. I am sure to include any and all links that I deem necessary for a careful analysis of the material contained in the unit. This works very well when presenting the creative naturalist sections. All works of artists, writers, poets, and researchers can be linked by the click of a button. It also proves quite helpful when linking to short videos, podcasts, or other types of media.

It must be noted that the school where I teach has developed a Web site that allows for teachers to post pages. If your school

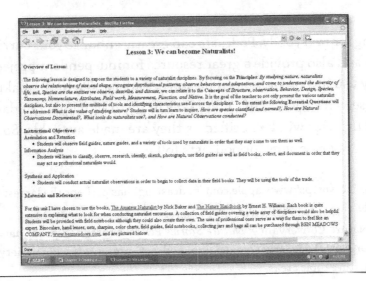

Figure 9. Lesson plan page on the author's Web site.

does not, there are many free sites that offer templates for educators to develop and use. Most eliminate the need for knowledge of HTML and Web authoring. You simply select a template and you are all set to create a Web site for your students.

Tripod (http://www.tripod.lycos.com) is a great site to begin your design. You will find it very user-friendly. As with any free program, keep in mind that space is limited and your Web site will be in the public domain.

There are many additional Web site features I have yet to employ. You could add blogs, a forum environment, and set up an e-mail service as well. As long as information can be linked, your Web site can contain a wealth of these resources.

Podcasts

Podcasts provide a wonderful opportunity for students to hear information from trusted and knowledgeable online sources. The great variety of them ensures that there is something for everybody. Podcasts can greatly enhance your curriculum and also provide a great resource for independent projects. They usually are organized by subject area and length, making the search easier. Many sites allow users to sign up for updates and the user will be notified as they are made available. Some of my favorite sites for podcasts follow.

Apple Inc. (http://www.apple.com/podcasting) has perhaps the largest collection of free subscriptions.

The Nature Conservancy: *Nature Stories* Podcast (http://support.nature.org/site/PageServer?pagename=podcast) presents a wide variety of nature topic areas.

Nature Podcast (http://www.nature.com/nature/podcast/index.html) offers podcasts from the weekly journal, *Nature*.

National Public Radio (http://www.npr.org) contains a wealth of resources, including their Friday afternoon program, Science Friday. Each broadcast is supplemented with a series of educator resources. Sometimes, I simply turn it on and have the students listen. Past programs are archived as podcasts.

Open Culture (http://www.oculture.com/2006/10/university_podc.html) has compiled a huge list of colleges and universities providing lectures in a podcast audio format. Hearing it from the experts in the field is the best resource for projects and enhancing understanding.

Virtual Field Trips

For those times when you simply cannot get away, it is easy to bring that far away place to you. Collected below is a list of some virtual fieldtrips.

All Along a River (http://library.thinkquest.org/28022/?tqskip1=1&tqtime=1024) offers students a chance to explore the physical properties of rivers, including case studies of the Singapore River and the Rhine.

EFISH: The Virtual Aquarium (http://www.cnr.vt.edu/efish/index.html) is maintained by the Department of Fisheries and Wildlife Sciences at Virginia Tech University.

Geology Virtual Field Trip links (http://www.uh.edu/~jbutler/anon/anontrips.html) are offered on this site from the geology department at the University of Houston.

Glacier National Park Electronic Field Trip (http://www.sd5.k12.mt.us/glaciereft/atour.htm) includes both pictures and audio for your students to explore the park.

Green Mountain Audubon Society (http://greenmountainaudubon.org) offers a virtual tour of its grounds, flora, and birdlife.

Mooloolah State School's Rainforest Tour (http://www.schools.ash.org.au/mooloolah/location/moololahss.html) allows students to explore the rainforest that was planted and has been maintained by students of Mooloolah State School since 1988.

The National Zoo (http://nationalzoo.si.edu) allows students to learn about the animals at the zoo, including great cats, invertebrates, reptiles, and great apes.

Saudi Arabian Hot Spots for Birding (http://www.camacdonald.com/birding/mesaudiarabia.htm) allows your young ornithologists to explore the birdlife of the Arabian Peninsula.

Virtual Tidepool (http://www.ocparks.com/tidepools/tidepool.htm), courtesy of the Crystal Cove Conservancy, allows students to explore animals and plants that call tidepools home.

Wild Sanctuary (http://earth.wildsanctuary.com) is home to one of the largest private archive of natural sound. Use Google Earth or Google Maps to search for specific sounds of habitats and animals. Each entry displays field study data taken during the recording.

Video

I tend not to be the type of educator who sets up the DVD player and lets it roll for the duration of the class. However, in this digital media age of YouTube and the like, there are small segments of video out there that provide excellent resources for you and your students. Of course, it is as easy as typing in a search at Google Video, but if you want some reputable sites to begin with, here is a list of some that I turn to regularly.

Discovery Education Streaming (http://streaming.discoveryeducation.com/index.cfm) provides a streaming video service, but requires a login. Most schools and libraries have access to this outstanding archive.

National Geographic (http://video.nationalgeographic.com/video): What's better than flipping through the pages of the latest *National Geographic* magazine? Well, viewing the amazing videos they stream online.

Nature (http://www.pbs.org/wnet/nature/video.html), the Public Broadcasting Service show, is archived on the PBS Web site, which also includes teacher resources.

Speakers

Over the years I have invited various speakers into my classroom as a way to enhance the curriculum. Many professors and graduate students love to share the information they have with younger pupils. Make contact with your local college or university to arrange a time to have a speaker visit your class. Most often, they will bring tools, share their research, and offer time for students to ask questions. They sometimes will be willing to serve as mentors to students completing independent projects.

Ask a Naturalist

In addition, many Web sites offer a chance for the general community to pose questions to an expert in the field. An archive of previously asked questions along with their answers is usually kept. Some of the sites I find helpful include the following.

Ask-a-Geologist: http://walrus.wr.usgs.gov/ask-a-geologist

Ask-a-Biologist: http://www.askabiologist.org.uk/punbb/viewtopic. php?id=758

Ask-a-Botanist: http://askabiologist.asu.edu/profiles/landrum/index.html

Birdchat (ornithologists): http://www.ornithology.com/chat.html

Ask-a-Marine Scientist: http://oceanlink.island.net/biodiversity/ask/ask. html

I also have had students in the past contact university researchers directly. If students come across a name of an individual who does work in a particular field on a Web site or in a journal article, newspaper, or magazine, encourage them to contact the individual directly via mail or e-mail. After a short lesson on letter and e-mail etiquette, I often am surprised by the quick and personal responses that some of my students receive from world-renowned experts in the field.

Other Web Sites of Interest

AllNature.org (http://www.allnature.org) allows students to view and post their own nature photos.

Animal Diversity Web (http://animaldiversity.ummz.umich.edu/site/index. html) includes firsthand identification and classification of species for the student or professional.

Basics of Tree ID (http://www.cnr.vt.edu/dendro/Forsite/Idtree.htm) is a basic guide to identifying trees and describing leaves, fruits, and barks, with many images.

Catalogue of Life (http://www.catalogueoflife.org/search.php) presents a searchable database of the world's species.

The Children & Nature Network (http://www.cnaturenet.org) encourages and supports the people and organizations working to reconnect children with nature.

eNature (http://www.enature.com) contains a variety of nature related-
photos, an ask an expert section, and more. Students also can sign up
for e-mail updates.

International Field Guides (http://www.library.uiuc.edu/bix/fieldguides/
main.htm) contains information on field guides from around the world
including where to get them and how much they cost.

Mammal Species of the World (http://invertebrates.si.edu/mammals/msw)
includes a searchable list of the world's mammal species.

Museum of Comparative Zoology at Harvard University (http://mcz-28168.
oeb.harvard.edu/mcztypedb.htm) includes a database of insects that
hosts a wealth of information.

NatureServe (http://www.natureserve.org/getData/index.jsp) is a conservation database for the United States, Latin America, and Canada.

Naturesongs (http://www.naturesongs.com) provides samples of various
natural sounds and photos, promotes nature recording and archiving,
and provides a library of sounds that people can refer to when they
hear something new.

NatureSound Studio (http://www.naturesound.com) offers a wealth of
nature sounds and recordings.

The Rock Identification Key (http://www.minsocam.org/msa/collectors_
corner/id/rock_key.htm) includes a database of rock types and
identification.

Tree of Life (http://tolweb.org/tree/phylogeny.html) is compiled by biolo-
gists and presents more than 9,000 species on Earth, illustrating the
diversity of life.

USGS Bird ID Page (http://www.mbr-pwrc.usgs.gov/bbs/ident.html) is
a guide to identifying the birds of North and Central America that
includes sound clips of bird songs.

Summer Opportunities for Teachers

For those of you who wish to become immersed in the field
of natural studies, many colleges, universities, and organizations offer summer courses and programs for teachers. I have

compiled a list below of some of the ones I have come across. There also is an excellent book by Jill Frankfort titled *100 Paid Summer Adventures for Teachers* that presents opportunities that are free for educators and, in most cases, offer a stipend to the participant. It can be found online at http://www.benefitpress.com.

ARMADA Project (http://www.armadaproject.org) provides K–12 teachers an opportunity to actively participate in ocean, polar, and environmental science research and peer mentoring.

Audubon Society (http://www.audubon.org/educate/cw/index.php) hosts ecology camps and workshops organized by state.

College of the Atlantic Teacher Summer Courses (http://www.coa.edu/html/coursesk12teachers.htm) is a program for K–12 teachers. Courses are offered on fieldwork, lab or studio sessions, and seminar discussions.

Earthwatch Institute (http://www.earthwatch.org/expedition) offers worldwide 1- and 2-week field study programs with scientists in the areas of oceans, endangered ecosystems, biodiversity, cultural diversity, sustainability, global change, and world health. Grants are available for K–12 teachers.

National Association of Geoscience Teachers Program (http://www.nagt.org/nagt/programs/usgs_field.html) offers field geology opportunities for teachers.

NOAA Teacher at Sea (http://teacheratsea.noaa.gov) looks for motivated teachers with a desire to do scientific research at sea and share that experience with students and colleagues.

Smithsonian National Zoological Park & Conservation Research Center Teacher Workshops (http://nationalzoo.si.edu/education/teacherworkshops) offer several courses throughout the year concerning to a variety of subjects related to field studies.

Chapter 10

Conclusion

Setting your students free from how they traditionally think about science is a gift they will cherish. Simply bringing your students out into the field to put into practice one lesson learned in the classroom will go a long way in helping achieve this. However, in pursuing a whole unit that embraces the world outside the classroom walls, more preparation is necessary. In order to help ensure your success during this course of instruction, I would like to share a few final thoughts, with the hope that you experience the excitement that will come from instructing your students to become naturalists.

1. Feel free to modify and personalize the unit.

    What I have offered here is only the suggestion of a sequence of lessons and experiences. During the years I've used this material, I have found myself teaching lessons completely out of order. Sometimes I begin with observation; other times I use the history of the field as a starting point. There have been times when

I spend more time in one area than I expected to and other times when the students seem to fly through the material. I have substituted index cards for project sheets, shifted oral presentations to other topics, and added and dropped a variety of lessons.

That is the freedom that comes from teaching the naturalist discipline. You have to "go with the flow." The students will let you know when they are ready to move on. As with any unit of instruction, it is the journey more than the destination. I can only take the students as far as they will go. You also will need to judge how far you want to take the material. Some students will excel, becoming experts, while others will be content with simple identification. The importance comes from the simple eye-opening realization of the discipline itself.

2. Don't be afraid to say, "I don't know."

Even though I have a background in the naturalist field, there are many days when I have to say, "I don't know." In the immense body of knowledge that exists, there will always be room for new knowledge acquisition. The students respect this attitude from the educator and in turn learn to uncover information for themselves. You will come to find information in this way as well. The material is there and only needs to be found.

3. Seek out your own resources.

As I write this final chapter, I am constantly reminded of the many resources I did not include in this text. Once your eyes are open to the field, you will begin to see the discipline everywhere. Every magazine I open, newspaper I read, television program I watch, and radio station

There is nothing more rewarding than watching students becom naturalists.

I listen to seems to be calling out for content connection. A simple stroll down the road will get your mind racing. Become an information gatherer. Keep a notebook or small pad around and jot down your ideas. Make the unit your own and utilize the resources you are most comfortable with. The naturalist discipline involves all we do. Geography and nature dictate many of the cultural values and markers that exist in society for you and your students. That is perhaps the strongest realization for them.

I wish you success as you pursue this course of instruction. I hope that the ideas, resources, and lessons will help guide your work. The students in your classroom are the future leaders and stewards of this planet. Using this material will bring them a step closer to nature and teach them respect, patience, appreciation, and expression at the same time. I look forward to hearing from you, the readers. Feel free to contact me at jdanielian@nagc. org with any ideas, opinions, suggestions, or comments.

Have fun!

Resources Supporting Natural Science Education

What follows is a selection of research articles that support this view of teaching and enriching the young naturalist, just in case anyone wonders what it is you are doing there in your classroom.

Akerson, V. L., Flick, L. B., & Lederman, N. G. (2000). The influence of primary children's ideas in science on teaching practice. *Journal of Research in Science Teaching, 37*, 363–385.

Elliot, D. L., Nagel, K. C., & Woodward, A. (1986). Scientific illiteracy in elementary school science textbook programmes. *Journal of Curriculum Studies, 19*, 73–76.

Feller, B. (2004, July 4). Teachers warn science education not making the grade. *The Providence Journal*, p. A3.

Hogan, K. (2000). Exploring a process view of students' knowledge about the nature of science. *Science Education, 84*, 51–70.

Louv, R. (2005). *Last child in the woods: Saving our children from nature deficit disorder.* Chapel Hill, NC: Algonquin Books.

Massey, C. (2000). *Science learning in the 21st century: A perspective from cognitive science.* Unpublished thesis, University of Pennsylvania, Philadelphia.

Osborne, J., Collins, S., Ratcliffe, M., Millar, R., & Duschl, R. (2003). What "ideas-about-science" should be taught in school science? A Delphi study of the expert community. *Journal of Research in Science Teaching, 40,* 692–720.

Renzulli, J. S., Leppien, J. H., & Hays, T. S. (2000). *The multiple menu model: A practical guide for developing differentiated curriculum.* Mansfield Center, CT: Creative Learning Press.

Schenkel, L. A. (2002). Hands on and feet first: Linking high-ability students to marine scientists. *Journal of Secondary Gifted Education, 13,* 173–191.

Stake, J. E., & Mares, K. R. (2001). Science enrichment programs for gifted high school girls and boys: Predictors of program impact on science confidence and motivation. *Journal of Research in Science Teaching, 38,* 1065–1088.

About the Author

Jeff Danielian is a middle school teacher of natural science in Providence, RI. He received his bachelor's degree in natural science from Lyndon State College in the Northeast Kingdom of Vermont and his master's degree in educational psychology from the University of Connecticut. Jeff currently is the Gifted Resource Specialist for the National Association for Gifted Children, working from his Rhode Island home on many exciting projects, including being editor-in-chief of *Teaching for High Potential*. He has presented at local, national, and international conferences on teaching the naturalist curriculum and a variety of other topics.

Printed in the United States
by Baker & Taylor Publisher Services

Printed in the United States
by Baker & Taylor Publisher Services